THIS MURDEROUS BUSINESS

THIS MURDEROUS BUSINESS

Murder, riot and fraud in old Argyll

Lindsay Campbell

T

Troubador Publishing Ltd
Unit E2 Airfield Business Park,
Harrison Road, Market Harborough,
Leicestershire. LE16 7UL
Tel: 0116 2792299
Email: books@troubador.co.uk
Web: www.troubador.co.uk

ISBN 978 1805142 911

British Library Cataloguing in Publication Data.
A catalogue record for this book is available from the British Library.

Printed and bound in Great Britain by 4edge Limited
Typeset in 11pt Adobe Garamond Pro by Troubador Publishing Ltd, Leicester, UK

ACKNOWLEDGEMENTS

Grateful thanks are due to the following people whose input to the research and writing of this work has been invaluable:

The staff of Oban Library.

Jackie Davenport and Rory Crutchfield at Argyll and Bute County Archives ("Live Argyll")

Alison Diamond and the volunteers of The Argyll Papers.

The staff of the Historic Search Room, National Records of Scotland, Edinburgh.

The volunteers of the Slate Islands Museum and Heritage Trust.

The volunteers of the Glasgow Police Museum; Liam Bowler, Metropolitan Police Heritage Service; Bob Clark, Rachael Thomas and the volunteers at Auchindrain Township Museum; Malcolm Ogilvie and Ray Lafferty from The Museum of Islay Life; K. Lindsay at the Oban Beer Seller; Marian Pallister; Nickie Sweeney at Angler's Corner; Colin and Flora Winter at Shellacan; Grace Woolmer at Perth & Kinross Heritage Trust,

Mr. Jeremy Thompson, Hannah Dakin, Lauren Bailey, Holly Porter, Raisa Patel, Chelsea Taylor, Chloe Messinger and all the staff at Troubador.

and especially my nonagenarian proof-reader!

ONE

It probably wasn't an unusual sight to the early 19th century inhabitants of the county town of Inveraray in Argyll; the people of that busy little town on the edge of Loch Fyne may have seen prisoners being escorted to kirk on a Sunday morning more than once. The sight however that summer morning in 1820, must have turned a few heads as the group of convicted prisoners and debtors walked, probably shackled, down Main street from the old jail. This latter place had been built 65 years before, when the Jacobite Rebellion was still fresh in everyone's minds, when the soldiers who fought in it and still bore the scars, later built the new roads and bridges throughout the Duke's estates, and when the economy was reeling from the battering it (and the people) had received as a result of the political upheaval.[1]

That old jail of 1755 soon became notorious for being cold, damp and unsanitary. It had had problems from the day it was built, when prison bars weren't fixed, windows leaked and not even the foundations were problem-free. [2] When the Circuit Court visited, as it did a few times a year to hear the serious cases of murder, forgery, treason or piracy which the Sheriff, or other local courts weren't authorised to hear, they stayed in the New Inn over the road, and processed in all their glory to the Court room on the first storey of the jail.[3] By 1820, there'd been discussions to replace the old jail for many years,[5] even before the new town was built around it on the Rudha-na-h-Airde promontory, but the miserable prisoners had a long time to wait for such an event.

That summer morning in 1820 though, they were being walked, guarded by halbadiers, from their old jail for the last time. This time, they weren't being walked to kirk; their destination was to a headland in the western half of the town, where a sturdy new edifice awaited them. A new jail and a new court house had been built there, the one a suitably ominous structure standing independently four-square, with two storeys comprising cold, windowed cells on each floor, stone stairs, and the most basic of sanitary provisions. Over at the new court house, apart from various service rooms for staff and guards, there were cells on the ground floor originally for all but the debtor-prisoners (men, women, children and the insane), tucked below an imposing semi-circular court room, to which prisoners would be conveyed up yet another stone stairway to the dock. Coming from the dark of that winding stair into the openness of the court room, wood panelled and with an auditorium of seating all round, must have been more than daunting. Before the court-room, the Fiscal, Sheriff or whoever was in charge of proceedings sat on his own podium behind a desk and with the Royal Coat of Arms above him on the wall. Opposite, tall windows looked out to the loch, and one can't help but pick up an atmosphere in there even today, set out as it is now, as a tableau of the past.[7]

Among the prisoners who would have been transferred to this fine new jail on the headland at the edge of the town, were Lachlan MacMillan from South Knapdale parish, found guilty by his own confession of hamesucken (breaking, entering and assaulting) at the spring Circuit Court and sentenced to twelve months behind bars.[8] There were a couple of thieves who also pled guilty,[9] and doubtless a clutch of debtors, just serving their time repaying what they owed someone else. There would have been numerous other prisoners but for the fact that some were held in Campbeltown, while many of them absconded from the law, going outlaw, probably under the impression that a hanging awaited them.[10] But for a Royal pardon, there would have been a hanging only nine years previously,[11] and the spectre of such doom laden occasions probably still haunted the minds of Argyll folk. As it happens, there weren't to be any more hangings in Inveraray's history.

The lack of hangings at Inveraray was undoubtedly fortunate for one of the prisoners in the line up being walked to the new jail, and this was a man from Kilchrenan, the remaining participant in a riot there.[12] There was also 28 year old Malcolm MacTaggart from Islay, who had another few months to serve, and had been convicted of culpable homicide to a mature widow the previous year.

At the time Islay was a hotbed of illegal distilling,[14] and one day in 1819, some Mullaich had arrived to do business at Loch Gruinart's illicit whisky still. Malcolm had been there helping the Mullaich at the time, (and of course helping himself to the products of the still) and there may have been a sword handy for when the Excise came a-calling.[15] After their visitors had loaded up the boat, Malcolm saw the men off, and someone went to guide the vessel through the difficult channel of Loch Grunairt, shallow as it was at the best of times, but with the tide only just coming in, even more difficult to manoeuvre.[16]

The previous day, Malcolm had met a local widow, Katie MacAulay, at his father-in-law's house at Killinallan.[17] Katie and her late husband had been married for thirty years, but it seems had never had any children,[18] and Malcolm was very friendly with her, old enough to be his mother as she was; he later said he couldn't remember seeing her at all after meeting her at his father-in-law's. After seeing the Mull men off, the next thing Malcolm remembers he was at Alex MacMillan's house, also at Killinallan, to pick up one of his children whom he'd deposited there, presumably for safety while he was at the still-house.[19] Malcolm chatted with Alex and his wife, then he and the wee boy went home, where his wife didn't seem to be around, and no-one seemed to have spoken to him on the way. Going inside, he didn't bother getting changed for bed, and just fell asleep in his clothes. [21] What happened to wee Angus he didn't say, but he himself apparently slept the sleep of the inebriated that night.

Malcolm woke the following morning at his usual time, to find himself still in his day clothes, bone dry, and someone knocking on his door. At the door when Malcolm went to open it was his half brother Angus MacDougall. There was bad news; Katie MacAulay had been found dead on the sands (the "merse") by Loch Gruinart, terribly cut about the head with severe wounds in a "barbarous and savage" attack by someone with a "sharp edged or lethal weapon" in a murder for which all the locals were laying the blame on Malcolm, threatening to even kill him in his bed, without benefit of judge or jury. Malcolm told his half brother that he couldn't possibly have killed Katie MacAulay, since he'd never born her any ill will, although he did begin to wonder where he'd been the previous evening, between leaving the MacMillan's house and arriving home; he couldn't remember anything from that time and Angus senior didn't tell him anything else.[22]

Strangely, as Malcolm's half brother turned away, another local on the farm, the tailor Archie Ferguson was standing outside his own house, not saying a word. He wasn't the only one who wouldn't meet and speak to Malcolm that day, since after telling his wife about Katie's death, and leaving home to go to his Dad's cottage at Corsapul, he found his father's family still apparently asleep, which at that time in a morning (about 6am) for a farmer in summer was unusual. Did they see Malcolm coming down the path from Bunanuillt and not want to get involved, so pretended to be still asleep?

Infact the only person who would speak to Malcolm was coming down the hill at that moment; another half brother, Gilbert, it seems hadn't heard about the tragedy on the loch shore, and Malcolm himself had to tell him everything he'd heard. Perhaps wisely, Gilbert took Malcolm to his own house, where he stayed for the remainder of the day.

Come evening, Malcolm left his half-brother's house and went to get the ferry over to Jura. He slept somewhere on Jura that night (it isn't specified where) before heading for the mainland. He didn't have any employment on Islay at the time, and in a move not uncommon then, but which set in the context of Katie MacAulay's death, seems rather suspicious, he ended up at Kilbarchen in Renfrewshire,[23] where he managed to get a job. There, Malcolm MacTaggart stayed for the rest of the season, until November, when he decided it was time to face the music back on Islay. Had he begun to remember things from that missing period between leaving the MacMillans and arriving home, or had he just hoped (he seemed a rather 'simple' soul) that the locals would have forgotten, or at least forgiven him?[25]

Whatever his cause, he arrived back home on Islay and proceeded to make his way to the local JP's house, Dr. Crawford. While he'd been away, a warrant for his arrest had been issued and the authorities were looking for him. Consequently, Malcolm didn't get to the JP's house before someone noticed him, and a few days later he was on his way to jail in Campbeltown. It was in the Campbeltown tolbooth where Malcolm MacTaggart made his first statement, translated from his Islay Gaelic by a local lawyer. Malcolm then faced a winter in Campbeltown tolbooth, awaiting transferral to Inveraray, presumably when someone there had received notice of the Circuit Court's visit. One April day, he was taken from his cell in the tolbooth, up to Inveraray, perhaps by boat, to be lodged in the damp, dark and cold murderer's cell in the old jail. One can only guess at his feelings at this stage; with the possiblity of a hanging if he was guilty, or the prospect of several more terrible months in the hellhole of the big murderer's cell below the court room, one can understand why he chose to plead Not Guilty, whether he remembered anything about the incident on Loch Gruinart shore or not.[26]

Malcolm MacTaggart's trial that April day in Inveraray would have been one of the last High Court trials in the building, and it was before Advocate Depute Menzies and

Lord Gillies that Malcolm reiterated what he remembered of those days just before and after the death of Katie MacAulay; that he didn't remember seeing her on the day she was found dead, only the day before when he'd met her at his father-in-law's, that he had "a very great regard" for her, and that he'd left Islay to find work, not to flee as a guilty man.[27]

The list of witnesses for Malcolm's trial is suitably long, with the names of many locals at Bunanuillt and Killinallan, along with curiously, a pedlar.[28] Had he been the one to find Katie's body? The Mullaich are also listed as witnesses (Islay whisky, technically still illicit, was often viewed as almost tax exempt ; nevertheless it seems the Mullaich rightly considered it more important that a suspected murderer be prosecuted than they risk being fined themselves)[29]. A local doctor is also on the witness list, so there may have been some sort of autopsy for Katie.[30] Unfortunately, the witness statements are missing from the trial notes, either being part of the paperwork lost in a fire at the clerk's chambers a few years later,[31] or perhaps not even written down at the time, simply listened to and considered as the witness spoke their testimony in court.

Whatever those witnesses told or wrote of the tragedy, Malcolm was eventually found not guilty of murder, but guilty of culpable homicide, giving him twelve more months to spend behind bars at Inveraray.[32] Of course only four or five of those were spent in the old jail, and he was one of those who must have felt some relief at being lodged in a small but dry, and clean cell in the new structure, even though the window was still barred.

With the lack of written witness statements in Malcolm's trial, it's difficult to come to any conclusion about whether he truly did kill Katie MacAulay. A few things do stand out though, even without any witness statements or an autopsy report.

For Katie to have wounds on her head, but crucially not on her neck (other cases are all too ready to quote neck and shoulder injuries, so if there'd been any, it's likely to have been mentioned), she must have been sitting down at the time, or at least significantly lower than her attacker. Without any quoted injuries to her hands or arms, it doesn't look as if she was able to raise her arms to defend herself, so the first hit must have been pretty vicious, and knocked her out, unless of course she was already asleep or blind drunk, perhaps half lying down on the merse. Unless she was asleep or drunk, whoever had attacked her must have crept up quietly, or else she'd have certainly heard them, tried to stand up or at least raised her arms to defend herself.

The other question that arises is how did the locals know it had been Malcolm who'd attacked her? If he'd been seen actually attacking her, then why did no-one intervene, or if they'd been too scared and felt vulnerable themselves (maybe Malcolm's wife, or another woman) they clearly didn't go to Katie immediately Malcolm had left the scene, otherwise she wouldn't have been simply found dead, but spoken of as found dying after the attack? Clearly no-one else had been present at the time of the attack, nor immediately afterwards. So how do the locals know Malcolm was the guilty party? Had he been seen arguing with Katie sometime before, perhaps near the whisky still; had Katie been wanting a share in the whisky and Malcolm had refused, or had she been haranging him for getting drunk while he had care of his wee boy? Was he still carrying the sword, suitably bloodied, later on when someone did see him before he went to his house. His clothes can't have been excessively bloodied, or else someone would have commented, and it's not an unusual scenario for an attacker's clothes to not bear huge blood stains in such an attack,[33] especially one could imagine outdoors where eg.bloodied door frames wouldn't smear sleeves as the attacker left through them.

Malcolm's own testimony, naturally, doesn't give any hint as to the truth of the story, if indeed there is any other truth than what he gave account of. The only query which does arise, is that if he'd been as drunk on whisky as he said he was, could he have been capable of inflicting such deadly accurate injuries on Katie? The whole impression one gets when reading through the entire trial notes is that either Malcolm wasn't as drunk as he claimed he was, or he was downright lying. Someone else may have kept a secret of some sort in the whole tragic incident, but it does appear that Malcolm MacTaggart the unemployed farmer's son from the shores of Loch Gruinart, was responsible for widow MacAulay's death, whether that was intended as murder, or just culpable homicide.

As for the future of Malcolm and his immediate family after the tragedy, it seems that he returned to Islay after his time in the new Inveraray jail, as he and his wife had at least two more children after he was released, in addition to the two boys and a baby they'd had when he was jailed. They had however moved to an adjoining parish.[34] The children variously grew up and had children and grandchildren of their own[35], but the mystery is what eventually happened to Malcolm. He and his wife were obviously dead by the time his eldest son died,[36] and the men of that name living on Islay in 1841, are totally unlike Malcolm in age and offspring.[37] It may be that Malcolm and his wife emigrated or moved south or to Ireland, and there disappeared into history, Malcolm's doubtful reputation suitably hidden in an anonymous new location.

Apart from Malcolm MacTaggart, one of the other prisoners who'd been walked to the new prison at Inveraray in summer 1820, had been Alexander MacDougall, a young disabled man from Kilchrenan parish, who'd been involved in what at the time appears to have been taken as two disturbing riots surrounding the capture of some illicit whisky.

There was a lot of social and political tension in the country at the time. After the Napoleonic wars, and the resulting economic downturn, the first stirrings of the Industrial Revolution also caused the first stirrings of a workers' rebellion. Committees were set up, strikes planned, placards and posters advertised the rebellion, and the protests and riots soon started.[39] The authorities in Glasgow especially were under high tension[40] and the government's response was unequivocal: the militia was called out, government spies sent among the rioting rebels, with arrests eventually being made, and men being hanged then beheaded.[41] In Inveraray, the Council sent a letter of support to the king, and advised householders and parents to keep their servants and children indoors on the days of the proposed workers' strikes and protests. The Town Crier read out warnings, the town drums were locked away and despite the posters popping up around the town, the militia and parish constables managed to keep everything under control.[43]

Naturally, any sign of unrest and local tension anywhere in Argyll at the time was going to be dealt with pretty harshly, so when word was received that the Excise might have problems handling a haul of illicit whisky at Kilchrenan, the authorities made arrangements to come down heavily on all concerned.

In the days prior to the Excise's assault on Kilchrenan parish, there were hints that someone had passed information to a local exciseman; he was advised to keep out of the way or at least wear a white coat, so that the illegal distillers would know not to attack him in any ensuing riot. Soon after, the expected party of Excise, led by James Inglis from Oban, travelled to Kilchrenan, heading straight for the house occupied by Peter Gardner at Collaig. There, they found two 8 gallon casks of whisky, which they 'gauged', along with some malt also in the house, and loaded it all up, presumably on a pony and cart for transfer to Kilchrenan. Alex MacDougall, who happened to be at Gardner's house at the time, claimed the casks and malt were his, and would gladly go with the Excise to pay the duty on them as required.[44] So onto Kilchrenan the small party went, aiming for the change house and inn run by the recently widowed Ann MacCall.[45] There has long been a tradition in Kilchrenan about one visit the Excise made to this same inn, when they stashed a cask of illicit whisky in an upstairs room, leaving one of their number sitting on the cask for safety. On that occasion however the Kilchrenan distillers weren't so easily put off and someone managed to drill a hole through the floor below into the whisky cask and draw off the contents, leaving the Excise with an empty cask.[46] Whether this tradition ties in with the Excise raid of 1820 is unknown as there isn't any mention in the trial notes of such behaviour, but if it did happen on this occasion, the distillers may have got their whisky, but it didn't affect the outcome of the case, since the Excise had already measured, assessed and noted the contents. The tradition may reflect an earlier incident, perhaps when the Excise weren't so wise as to do their gauging before they moved the casks from the original hiding place!

Whatever the circumstances of the Excise raid of 1820, once James Inglis' men got the casks to Kilchrenan, they left them in the stable and went to the inn itself, presumably to see to the paperwork which Alex MacDougall had said he was prepared to deal with. It was evening by then and it was in Ann MacCall's place that matters became violent. Other men were in the building when the Excise and Alex MacDougall arrived, which rather invites the assumption that Alex had been employed to tempt the Excise into walking straight into the resultant riot. Numerous men, some of them named, some "to the Prosecutor unknown" began attacking James Inglis and his men, using bludgeons, sticks and other weapons to strike and assault the Excise "to the effusion of blood" and "injury of persons", putting the excisemen in danger for their lives. Eventually, the attackers, perhaps not getting the success in the battle as they'd hoped, fled, leaving only Alex MacDougall to take the rap.

The Excise themselves it seems left the scene without apprehending Alex, as he was still living in the parish come the end of March when James Inglis decided to give Kilchrenan another go.[47] This time however, Inglis decided that he needed a bit more solid support than on his last foray into criminal-ridden Kilchrenan. He recruited some of the crew from an Oban-registered sloop, the Wellington, moored on Loch Etive and which he'd requisitioned for the cause (her normal run was Liverpool to Lisbon, so quite why she was back home in Oban is anyone's guess[48]). With the crew and other excisemen, Inglis and some 30 men, (including two officers from the ship), set off from Bonawe towards Kilchrenan. The parish boundaries of Inishail, Muckairn and Kilchrenan were rather convoluted at the time, meaning that although on the ground the route the men took is clear enough, the trial notes must have been confusing for any of the authorities outwith Argyll.

Perhaps because of this issue of parish boundaries, it was fairly early in this venture that James Inglis divided the group into two, sending one with the 2nd mate from the ship and one of the Excise officers to the vicinity of Barrachander, probably along the route of the modern road. Meanwhile, Inglis and the chief mate went with the remaining group to Shellacan, probably via the road from Fanans to do some more surveying, and hopefully catch the illicit distillers at work.[49] Alex MacDougall's own farm of Achnacraobh (not quite on its current site, but further north and closer to the road[50]) was next door to Barrachander, and as before, someone appears to have tipped the locals off. James Inglis perhaps sent a scout on ahead, and certainly there was a group of men waiting on the track to intercept the Excise. This time though Inglis wasn't going to be tempted into walking straight into the attack. On seeing, or perhaps hearing, that the attackers were waiting for them on the track round the other side of the hill, he withdrew his men back to wait for the other group to join them. Unfortunately, it turned out that he had to wait overnight, which in March can't have been a pleasant prospect. Perhaps they found some handy byre to shelter in, or perhaps they retired further back towards Fanans.[51]

Come the following day, Inglis and his men returned to their hiding place close to Shellacan, but unfortunately, the other group still didn't come to join them. There was only one thing Inglis could do; a battle had to be waged. Presumably emerging from their hiding place, Inglis, the sailors and the excisemen met the group of locals, armed with firearms, bludgeons, and broadswords, on and around the track and farmstead of Shellacan. Putting up the strongest of fights, Inglis' men waded into the fray, but received shots, strikes and wounds. Inglis himself was knocked to the ground and hit there repeatedly with a bludgeon, shot at, and his own staff ripped from his hands and used against him. It was only during this fight that the remaining group of excisemen and sailors reached Inglis and his men, undoubtedly hearing and seeing the fight going on from over at Barrachander, but all thirty of them got battered and assaulted, to the extent that with firearms going off, and the men risking their lives, Inglis wisely withdrew all his forces right back to Bonawe. As for the local men, in due course warrants were sent from Inveraray, but by then they'd all fled the scene, leaving only Alex MacDougall to face what may have been a hanging trial.[52]

With the workers' Rebellion still being waged across the country, there'd been an especially nasty battle in Glasgow just two and a half weeks after the Shellacan battle,[53] and it was only two days after that, that the authorities came with their warrant for the arrest of Alex MacDougall. Clearly someone, somewhere had a conviction that the Shellacan incident was associated more with the Rebellion than with rioting distillers, and they wanted Alex at least out of the way. So far out of the way infact that by summer, they'd sent him from Inveraray jail to Edinburgh, with everything gearing up for a treason case. Come the time of the opening of the new jail however, he was back in Argyll, awaiting his trial the following September, and the authorities must have realised that the fight on the road at Shellacan was no more than some hyped up locals defending their illicit still. A nasty, vicious, criminal assault certainly, (there was even reference in the Indictment papers to the 2nd Jacobite Rebellion) but not apparently part of the Radical Rebellion movement, and Alex got away with his life, the cases against two other (absent) rioters also being dismissed, whilst the remainder were declared outlaw, disappearing, like so many others, into history.[54]

Down at the now quiet parish of Kilchrenan, one thing is certain – just like on Islay where Malcolm MacTaggart's farmstead still stands, Barrachander still exists as a dwelling and a neat scatter of fanks and buildings by the road. Shellacan as it was in 1820 however survives only as clusters of half buried walls, lumps, bumps and outlines of dwellings with a fine house and a fine road replacing them the following century, whilst the road James Inglis took to sneak up on the distillers was walkable until recent years.[55]

There never were any real Rebellion protests in Argyll, for whatever reason. Argyll folk aren't quite the laid-back country yokels we're popularly assumed to be, but clearly at the time, there were more important things in their lives than political protest and strikes, and those people who first occupied the cells at the jail on Crown Point had greater things on their minds than the troubles of cash-strapped artisans in a city a hundred miles away.

FOOTNOTES

1. "Inveraray and the Dukes of Argyll" by Ian G. Lindsay and Mary Cosh published Edinburgh University Press 1973, pp.157-165.
2. Ibid., pp.162-4.
3. "Blood & Battery, murder, riot and theft in old Argyll" by Lindsay Campbell, published Troubador, Leicestershire, 2021, p.16 n47.
4. "Inveraray and the Dukes of Argyll" by Ian G. Lindsay and Mary Cosh published Edinburgh University Press 1973, pp.159,315-6.
5. Ibid., pp.315-318.
6. "Records of Argyll" by Lord Archibald Campbell, published Blackwood & sons, Edin 1885, p.49; "Inveraray and the Dukes of Argyll" by Ian G. Lindsay and Mary Cosh published Edinburgh University Press 1973, pp.12,15,25-26,27.
7. The Royal Commission on the Ancient and Historical Monuments of Scotland volume 7, Mid Argyll and Cowal, medieval and later monuments, published 1992, pp.445-448.
8. JC26/1820/131, available in the National Records of Scotland historic search room, Edinburgh.
9. Ibid.
10. Several criminals eg.Samuel Cuthbertson, JC26/1820/34, or two sheep stealers JC26/1820/131, and others, available in the National Records of Scotland historic search room, Edinburgh.
11. JC13/38/3, 1811; JC4/5,1811, pp.443b-445a; JC27/117 available in the National Records of Scotland historic search room, Edinburgh.
12. JC26/1820/42; JC13/48 available in the National Records of Scotland historic search room, Edinburgh.
13. JC13/47/63; JC26/1820/131 available in the National Records of Scotland historic search room, Edinburgh.
14. "Islay, biography of an island" by Margaret Storrie, published The Oa Press, 1997, pp.188-191.
15. "The Whisky Distilleries of the United Kingdom" by Alfred Barnard, published David & Charles Reprints, 1969, from original print of 1887, Introduction (no page references).
16. Testimony of Malcolm Ogilvie and Ray Lafferty from The Museum of Islay Life, to whom the author is indebted;

timeanddate.com; https://tides.willyweather.co.uk and a comparison of the tides on the nearest comparable moon phase in modern times, with the moon phase at the time of the murder.

17. JC13/47/63; JC26/1820/131, available in the National Records of Scotland historic search room, Edinburgh.

18. Marriages, Dec 1788, Bowmore parish, Old Parish Registers, available on scotlandspeople.com

19. JC13/47/63; JC26/1820/131, available in the National Records of Scotland historic search room, Edinburgh.

20. Baptisms, 1816, Bowmore parish, Old Parish Registers, available on scotlandspeople.com

21. JC13/47/63; JC26/1820/131, available in the National Records of Scotland historic search room, Edinburgh.

22. Ibid.

23. Ibid.

24. Baptisms, 1801, 1811, 1812 and others, Kilbarchen parish, Old Parish Registers, children of James, William and John Stevenson; the will of James Stevenson of Auchenames, Kilbarchen parish, available on scotlandspeople.com or www.ancestry.com

25. JC13/47/63; JC26/1820/131, available in the National Records of Scotland historic search room, Edinburgh.

26. Ibid.

27. Ibid.

28. Ibid.

29. Islay was unique in that in the post-Union days, the island retained the old system of relying on the lairds to collect distilling taxes, often of course resulting in numerous inefficiencies. Despite this system on Islay being ended by Malcolm MacTaggart's time, the habit of rampant illicit distillation continued, and there are many tales of the Excise being thwarted on Islay: "Islay, biography of an island" by Margaret Storrie, published The Oa Press, Islay 1997, pp.188-191.

30. JC13/47/63; JC26/1820/131, available in the National Records of Scotland historic search room, Edinburgh.

31. "Odd Incidents of Olden Times" or "Ancient Records of Inveraray", by Peter MacIntyre, published 1904, Aird and Coghill, Glasgow, p.9.

32. JC13/47/63; JC26/1820/131, available in the National Records of Scotland historic search room, Edinburgh.

33. Science.howstuffworks.com/bloodstain-pattern-analysis2.htm; https://forident.com./research-articles/arterial-bloodstain-patterns-on-clothing-an-interesting-case-linking-the-accused-to-the-scene/

34. Baptisms, 1814, 1816, 1819, 1822, 1826 and 1828, Bowmore parish, Old Parish Registers, available on the scotlandspeople. com

35. Neil (baptised 1819) and his brother Gilbert lived next door to each other in Coulabus for many years, their various children and grandchildren also appearing on the subsequent censuses for Coulabus and vicinity, available on the scotlandspeople.com

36. Gilbert's death certificate, 1891, Coulabus, available on the scotlandspeople.com

37. Census Return, 1841, Oa. Malcom McTaggart, 36 yrs, living with Martha McTaggart, 66 yrs available on the scotlandspeople.com

38. Census Return, 1841, Campbeltown; death of a 57yr old Malcolm MacTaggart, 1858, a clothier, son of a tailor, which if the informant on the death had been correct/honest, would make him too young anyway to be the Malcolm MacTaggart of the 1820 case.

39. "The Encyclopaedia of Scottish Executions, 1750-1963", by Alexander F.Young, published Eric Dobby Publishing Ltd, Kent 1998, pp.86-89; "The Royal Burgh of Inveraray by Alexander Fraser, published by The Saint Andrew Press, Edinburgh 1977, p.49-51; wikipedia.org/wiki/Radical_war

40. "The Royal Burgh of Inveraray by Alexander Fraser, published by The Saint Andrew Press, Edinburgh 1977, p.49.

41. "The Encyclopaedia of Scottish Executions, 1750-1963", by Alexander F.Young, published Eric Dobby Publishing Ltd, Kent 1998, pp.86-89; "The Royal Burgh of Inveraray by Alexander Fraser, published by The Saint Andrew Press, Edinburgh 1977 pp.49-52; wikipedia.org/wiki/Radical_war

42. "The Royal Burgh of Inveraray by Alexander Fraser, published by The Saint Andrew Press, Edinburgh 1977, p.52.

43. Ibid., pp.49,50.

44. JC26/1820/42; JC13/48, available in the National Records of Scotland historic search room, Edinburgh.

45. Referred to as MacCail, her husband's will is registered 31.3.1819, "Argyll Commissary Court, A Calendar of Testaments, Inventories, Commissary Processes, and other records 1700-1825" edited by Frank Bigwood, p.465.

46. "It's a Far Cry to Loch Awe, a personal and historical tour around Scotland's longest loch" by Charlie Mitchell, published Dalmally Historical Society, 2016, p.76.

47. JC26/1820/42; JC13/48, available in the National Records of Scotland historic search room, Edinburgh. Inglis was Supervisor of Excise at the time, married to a young Aberdeenshire

woman, and with their first baby, a wee girl (Census Return, 1841, Campbeltown parish, and baptisms July 1820, Kilmore and Kilbride parish, Old Parish Registers, available on the scotlandspeople.com) He appears to have been a very capable man, not easily put off by rioting distillers and he spent all his working life in Argyll before moving to his wife's home county where he died at a ripe old age. (Death certificate, Newhills, Aberdeenshire, 1870, aged 92yrs, registered May 1870 available on scotlandspeople.com).

48. archive.org/details/HECROSU1819/page/n567/mode/2up; there was however a 'Wellington', an Excise cutter from Campbeltown c.1825: "An historical and genealogical tour of Kilkerran Graveyard" by Angus Martin, published Kintyre Civic Society, 2006, p.3.
49. JC26/1820/42; JC13/48, available in the National Records of Scotland historic search room, Edinburgh.
50. Comparison of several old maps, eg.Arrowsmith's (1807), Langland's (1804), Roy's (c.1750) and the early Victorian OS maps compared with the modern (Pathfinder,1:25 000) map all of which appear to show that Achnacraobh was situated very close to the modern road, and distinctly not on the same site as the current buildings, which however may well have existed at the same time, the immediate area having numerous remains, as per testimony of Flora Winter, Shellacan. Maps available on maps.nls.uk/Scotland/index.html
51. JC26/1820/42; JC13/48, available in the National Records of Scotland historic search room, Edinburgh.
52. Ibid.
53. "The Encyclopaedia of Scottish Executions, 1750-1963", by Alexander F.Young, published Eric Dobby Publishing Ltd, Kent 1998, p.88.
54. JC26/1820/42; JC13/48, available in the National Records of Scotland historic search room, Edinburgh. There were three MacIntyre brothers involved in the riot, living at Barrachander, all of whom had their cases dismissed; JC26/1820/42; JC13/48, available in the National Records of Scotland historic search room, Edinburgh.
55. Testimony of Colin and Flora Winter, to whom the author is indebted for their hospitality and their immense local knowledge.

TWO

M odern tourism is of course a vital industry in the West Highlands, islands and Argyll, but apart from the occasional visit of well-heeled tourists in the early 19ᵗʰ century, it wasn't until the likes of Walter Scott's romantic novels, and the tartan-clad visit of George IV in 1822, that tourism really took off.[1] Naturally, travel at that time in Argyll was as difficult as it ever was, even with the military roads of two generations before, but the rise of steam power to fuel the wooden ships made sea travel easier and people began sailing to and from Glasgow and the south via the new steamers, stopping off at the likes of Tobermory or Dunoon.[2]

It wasn't only tourists on these early steam ships of course, and two travellers heading to Glasgow on the Maid of Islay in 1826 had boarded at Applecross in Inverness-shire. They were both Dingwall men and mildly acquainted with each other; one was Stewart Chisholm, a pernickety but happily married army surgeon in his thirties, father of three young children and apparently well respected in Inverness-shire.[3] The other man was Archie MacQueen, the son of a kirk minister at Applecross. MacQueen was a mature, unmarried legal man, and had served some time in Demerara on the plantations there; his brother was a surgeon with the East India Company and he had business connections in London and back home in Inverness-shire.[4]

On the day Chisholm and MacQueen boarded the ship, the former was heading to Canada with the regiment (the Royal Artillery), while the latter was heading down to London. On their way to Glasgow, the ship was due to make an overnight stop at Tobermory, which must have been a common occurrence at the time.[5] The little town had been an official government fishing station for decades by then, and a recognised sheltered anchorage for centuries with the older settlement up on the hill behind. There were a few streets and buildings, in the lower town at least, partly built on ground reclaimed from the shore, including cottages for the lower classes on the hill, and merchants' villas, public buildings, a kirk, pier, storage unit for the fishery, custom house and an inn. This latter was a two storey block on the sea front, and had served its time as accommodation for everyone from sailors to Circuit Court officials by then and would continue to do so for many years.[6]

When Chisholm and MacQueen's ship had moored at Tobermory's busy pier, the men obviously decided that they'd get some fresh air and stretch their legs before going to dinner at the inn, so they went to take a walk along the seafront. While they were out on the street, Chisholm noticed someone familiar ahead, walking arm in arm with another gentleman, and he pointed them out to MacQueen, who hadn't met the gentlemen before.[7]

Despite the presence of these two others, one of whom Chisholm clearly knew, the steam-ship travellers continued their walk, and so did the others. Infact the four of them walked so much that they passed each other twice on the street, and then a third time, before the other two men disappeared. At this point Chisholm asked MacQueen directly if he knew who the other man was; the latter must have had some considerable notoriety in the Dingwall area (and not in a good way!), but MacQueen said he didn't know him. Chisholm explained that he'd recently received a "vulgar" letter from "the notorious Frank MacKenzie", as part of an issue which he wasn't prepared to go into details about at the time, although he'd left the letter in the hands of the Inverness-shire Fiscal. This letter is currently untraceable in the old records, but it may have been deliberately well-hidden at the time in some obscure bundle now in Edinburgh. Modern historians can only guess at the contents, but they were clearly something judged at the time to be dishonourable and distasteful.

On the streets of Tobermory in 1826, and with MacKenzie and his companion gone inside, Chisholm and MacQueen also decided to retire to the New Inn to wait for dinner. Chisholm must have known that MacKenzie had gone there himself, since as soon as he was inside the Inn, the doctor called for pen, ink and paper and settled down to write a note; this one still exists, in the pack of old records in Edinburgh: "In your vulgar and blackguard's letter to me" Chisholm wrote, "you concluded by saying beware of me. Now sir, you cannot deny but that within the last quarter of an hour I have met you thrice. I am here still. Pray, what do you want of me?" Chisholm folded the note up, called over a servant girl and sent her with it to the adjoining room which he'd somehow learnt that MacKenzie was occupying.

Off the girl went with the note, only to promptly return; MacKenzie had refused to accept it. Chisholm took a look at the note and realised he hadn't met the expectations of etiquette and addressed it, so he did so, gave it to the servant again and sent her off with it a second time. Again the note came back, having been again refused by McKenzie.

By this time, MacQueen must have suspected that something other than a slavish insistence on etiquette was behind MacKenzie's repeated refusals of any communication from Dr. Chisholm, and he offered to take the note himself. Chisholm was already angry, and he really didn't want to send MacQueen to intercede, but eventually (perhaps thinking about MacQueen's legal training) he agreed, and handed him the note.

Probably not really knowing what he was getting involved in, Archie MacQueen read Dr. Chisholm's note himself then set off to deliver it. Frank MacKenzie and some other men were settled into the adjoining rooms at the New Inn, and when MacQueen arrived, he was shown into the bedroom there, where they were all gathered, in itself a rather strange location for a group of gentlemen to congregate socially. MacQueen doesn't appear to have been surprised however, and he asked Frank MacKenzie why he'd twice returned Chisholm's note, especially since it was now properly addressed. MacKenzie still declined to accept the note, even from MacQueen's hands, and he asked if it was in the role of a friend that MacQueen was delivering it. Quite what was meant by this question is difficult to understand, since what other role would MacQueen be serving, unless

MacKenzie assumed he was doing some legal work for Chisholm? Another curiosity is that MacQueen acted rather as if he was younger than Chisholm, serving him more like a younger brother rather than an older acquaintance. It could only therefore have been MacQueen's legal background which brought him into the argument, unless as a single man Chisholm thought that he could relate to MacKenzie, another single man, better.[8] It's at this point that something is hinted at in the old records, something which doesn't become evident until many years later. Frank MacKenzie was unmarried at the time,[9] which since he was only in his late twenties would have been perfectly acceptable. It was of course a standard expectation for a gentryman to marry, and was an expectation which would otherwise have been questioned, had he not eventually married, but with the group of gentlemen gathered in his bedroom, the one who'd been walking arm in arm with him earlier, and his close association in later life with another single gentleman, the (in)famous Dr. Liston, west coast rumours may have been rife about him. The whole issue is compounded for modern historians by an account of his death 18 years later, at the hands of this Dr. Liston, who is described in a biography written in Victorian times, as "an intimate personal friend" of his.[10] If such a phrase indicates something which at the time would have created huge scandal, it would have been wise for MacKenzie to be a little more subtle about his private life, even when away from home. Frank MacKenzie however clearly wasn't the sort to keep his private life private.

With the numerous gentlemen around him in his rooms at Tobermory Inn, and Archie MacQueen standing there with Dr. Chisholm's note, MacKenzie asked MacQueen another unusual question: what did he want from the doctor? A strange question to ask, which makes one wonder what MacKenzie expected MacQueen to want, but MacQueen said that he didn't want anything from him, he only wanted to know what MacKenzie had to say in reply to the note, seeing as the latter had previously threatened Chisholm.

At this point Frank MacKenzie must have realised that the man standing before him with the note knew about the "insolent" letter he'd sent to Chisholm, and he refused to speak to him any more. When pressed, he said that he'd send a friend with a message in response to the note before everyone retired to bed. MacQueen told him that he thought that would be satisfactory, and he left the room and returned to Chisholm, who seems to have been similarly satisfied.

And so the waiting started. Archie MacQueen and Stewart Chisholm sat waiting in the Inn at Tobermory "for some considerable time" for anyone to bring a message from Frank MacKenzie.

In fact they waited so long that Chisholm sent MacQueen to MacKenzie's room again to remind him. He must know, MacQueen told him, that the steamer was due to leave first thing in the morning, implying that there wouldn't be any chance for MacKenzie to send a message after breakfast. If he was going to send a friend with any message in response to the note, he'd better hurry up. Frank MacKenzie presumably heard MacQueen through, then simply turned round and walked away.

So the waiting continued; and continued. Eventually, with Chisholm probably livid by then, MacQueen went again to MacKenzie's rooms and found the latter in the corridor between the sitting room and the bedrooms.

They'd waited a considerable time now, he told him, and since no-one had arrived with the expected message, they wouldn't wait any longer. MacKenzie seemed unperturbed by this and simply repeated that they would have to wait his time, stating so "with a good deal of insolence in his manner and conversation".

It seems that it wasn't only Chisholm who was livid by now. Archie MacQueen told MacKenzie that he was a coward in refusing to converse with a man who had challenged him as Chisholm had done, but still MacKenzie wouldn't respond, just ignoring MacQueen and walking away again. MacQueen it seems followed him, probably still arguing, then, just before he went into his bedroom, Frank MacKenzie turned suddenly and kicked MacQueen, before running into the room, and presumably slamming the door. Archie MacQueen was not a coward however, and he burst into MacKenzie's bedroom, where he found him with four or five of the other gentlemen and landed him a right hook on his face. By this time, Dr. Chisholm had also come to MacKenzie's bedroom, and despite the greater number of men trying to defend the gentryman, the doctor and MacQueen landed out thumps, kicks and strikes on MacKenzie's body, including between his legs and various other places on his lower body. It took some effort on the part of MacKenzie's friends before they were able to separate the assailants from their target, and the latter was left badly injured.

Frank MacKenzie immediately took to his bed in the New Inn at Tobermory, and called in a local surgeon, Charlie Martin, who arrived to attend to the injured man that same morning. The Tobermory doctor found his patient with a "much battered" and swollen face, especially over his left eye and having lost some blood; Dr. Martin applied some leeches to the swellings, and cold lotions later on. MacKenzie can't have been too badly injured as he pretty quickly sent in a complaint to the Tobermory Fiscal, who set in motion the various necessities for raising a case of assault to the effusion of blood. Both Stewart Chisholm and Archie MacQueen were subsequently examined before a magistrate, but neither were arrested, and Chisholm continued on his way to Canada with the regiment.

Archie MacQueen meanwhile also continued on his way to London, conscientiously leaving a contact address for himself with the Fiscal. Some two months passed before MacQueen heard that a summons had been issued for his arrest, and, again, conscientiously, he made arrangements to leave London as soon as he could in order to attend the Fiscal's court. He arrived home in Dingwall a few weeks later to make a statement to the local sheriff, by which time he'd also informed the Argyll authorities that he was back in Scotland.

Meanwhile, over in Inveraray, things were moving as ponderously as usual, probably to the great annoyance of Frank MacKenzie. The biggest problem of course was that, whether Stewart Chisholm was abroad with the regiment or not, his home was well outwith the jurisdiction of the Inveraray courts. One can only imagine the headaches the lawyers in their new court house had, trying to get permission, warrants etc, to call up Dr. Chisholm to court at Inveraray, living as he did (when he was at home) in Ross-shire. Eventually these same lawyers managed to get the paperwork in order so they had the go-ahead to proceed with the case, and the summons was left at Dr. Chisholm's house in Strathglass. Everyone knew he was in Canada, so couldn't have attended just like that, but protocol had to be met anyway; his name was announced at the market cross and at the old tolbooth door as if he was a fugitive outlaw, running among the hills to escape the law.[11]

And there, as with so many cases brought to the Inveraray court, ends the legal arguing between Dr. Stewart Chisholm, the military surgeon and one Frank McKenzie of Dingwall. There was another argument brought to court where another surgeon, this time Dr. Lachlan McLean living on Rhum whose sister-in-law McKenzie had married, had an argument with the latter. The old records aren't fully clear on who had been persecuting whom, but less than a year after Dr. Chisholm's argument at Tobermory with McKenzie, Dr. McLean took out 'letters of horning' against McKenzie, summoning him to court to force him to repay a debt. They'd previously been friends, but now one of them was "unrelentingly" persecuting the other "in a spirit of oppression" and had been doing for the past three years. Crucially, for the way that Chisholm had landed some kicks in a sensitive part of McKenzie's anatomy, Dr. McLean really wasn't happy about McKenzie marrying his sister-in-law.[12] Had that spirit of fellowship common among ladies and gentlemen of the medical profession caused Chisholm to land out at McKenzie, in as much cause for the other doctor as for himself?

All this information about Frank McKenzie might indicate that his identity would be easy to pinpoint in the old records. Certainly it's easy to locate Dr. Chisholm and Archie MacQueen,[13] but perhaps considering McKenzie's escapades it's not surprising that he's almost impossible to pin down, at least using the middle name he'd clearly adopted by the time of the argument in the inn at Tobermory. The only Frank MacKenzie whom he could have been was the Dingwall gentryman, a baronet of Nova Scotia and a "kindly" man interested in agriculture and all county affairs, who escaped his bankruptcy debts to live in France, leaving his brother to handle his failing finance. He fathered three sons by two wives and died after being bled by that "intimate personal friend" in 1843.[14]

As for Archie MacQueen, the lawyer handy with a right hook, he went on to serve Demerara as an Advocate before returning to Britain and dying, still unmarried, and an Advocate in Law at Musselburgh at the age of 84.[15] The only one to come out of the whole messy business of the assault in the Tobermory Inn with any financial success in life, was Dr. Stewart Chisholm, who ended his days as a Surgeon Major in the Royal Artillery, with enough money to invest in quantities of silver cutlery and fine silver dinner sets. He'd travelled to Ceylon with the regiment it seems, had married well and had three or four children, each of whom he made sure received exactly the correct pieces from the dinner set after he died, and after settling back home in Inverness-shire had become a JP.[16] The incident in Tobermory it seems was never mentioned again, and the case may have been dismissed.

Over on the mainland just three years later, another doctor became involved in another violent incident. Dr. Malcolm MacLaurin was a Barcaldine born man, the son of a respectable tenant farmer, with four sisters; in his younger days he'd had an equally respectable job serving the Duke of Argyll as factor on Tiree. Unfortunately, although Dr. MacLaurin's job was respectable, he doesn't seem to have lived up to such respectability: he fathered two illegitimate children by two different local women and paid a heavy price for his profligacy; he lost his job and almost the roof over his head, and had to move to the mainland with his sisters, where he subsequently fathered a third illegitimate child.[17] By 1825, Dr. MacLaurin had settled in Oban, the thriving village at the edge of the Atlantic from where the new steamers plied their trade to and from Tobermory and other locations, while the summer visitors, on the back of tales by celebrity travel writers, were just beginning to realise the benefits of visiting the west coast. Dr. Malcolm MacLaurin had an income from his tenant farm at Ardentallen, while practising his trade in town, but like the Duke's tenantry on Tiree (along with the Duke himself and his staff[18]) he doesn't seem to have been popular among the Òbanaich.

At the time, Malcolm MacLaurin lived in a house at the northern end of town, just by Mr. Stevenson's Distillery and with a garden at the back, and views of the bay and George street at the front. The house is now The Oban Beer Seller,[19] and the slight slope of the land, now imperceptible, at the time seems to have resulted in MacLaurin's front parlour window being a few more feet above the pavement than would normally be the case. This, along with the presence of the Distillery and, it appears, quantities of "delinquents" roaming the Oban streets on an evening intent on enjoying themselves, resulted in the area infront of Dr. MacLaurin's window being a meeting place for the bored and unemployed youth of the village. Unfortunately, Dr. MacLaurin didn't look upon the bored and unemployed youth as being very respectable, and they consequently found great pleasure in poking fun at him, shouting abuse and incitements, having noisy conversations and arguments below his window, throwing mud and stones at his house and generally disturbing his peace. They cheered when a splat of mud hit the window, or jeered at him, making fun of his apparent snobbishness. They probably conversed in Gaelic, which may have increased MacLaurin's disturbance if he didn't have the tongue, not knowing what those rough delinquents were up to under his parlour window.[20]

Dr. Malcolm MacLaurin owned a shotgun. It was a fouling piece, with a long barrel, more properly used for shooting innocent ducks by means of small pieces of lead which scattered quite a distance,[21] in addition to annihilating any other wildlife within its range. One April day, when the ships in the bay had been firing their guns to acknowledge the king's birthday, MacLaurin decided to use this fouling piece against some sparrows in his back garden; the old phrase of using a mallet to crack a nut comes to mind, but when he'd finished this futile work, he evidently returned to his front parlour, where the usual congregation of delinquent youths were gathered in the street.[22]

Amongst these boys were young Archie Munn (a surname well familiar to modern Òbanaich), son of one of the workers at the distillery, and his friend John Campbell the Congregational minister's son.[23] There were other people around, perfectly self-respecting, if lowly, adults chatting or going about their equally respectable business. At some point, Dr. MacLaurin decided he'd had enough of the delinquents congregating below his window and took it upon himself to do something about it once and for all. Picking up his fouling gun, he opened his front parlour window and showed himself and the piece to the youths outside. 'Showed himself' isn't quite the correct description however, since with the size of the window, the length of the gun and the likelihood that the window was a sash and would therefore only open one half at any time, he would have had to put at least the barrel right out of the window for it to be visible.[24] Whatever he did with the gun, he said later that he called out for the boys to take care, but the youths were scared enough by the sight of the gun to immediately scatter to the four winds; Archie Munn and John Campbell ran round the corner into George street where a new terrace was being built. John was actually on an errand from his mother to pick something up at one of the shops further down the street, and with that excuse in mind, he cautiously emerged from hiding to see if MacLaurin and his gun had disappeared. Archie Munn stayed hidden. With "the good doctor" now out of sight, John Campbell called back to Archie and the latter emerged and went to stand near the water pump, in the middle of the street, but still within view of the parlour window.[25]

Dr. MacLaurin, still with the fouling gun in his hands inside his house, then decided that he needed to empty it, although quite why he decided to do so into the street he didn't say. Opening the window again, he fired the piece into the air, or so he later claimed. Again, the length of the gun, the ease of movement within the confines of the sash window and the layout of the street outside tell their own story. The spray of fine pellets from the gun would spread quite a distance[26] and it appears that MacLaurin was trying to aim approximately towards George street. It would have been impossible for him to aim squarely at young Archie Munn, now standing a bit nearer, but the spray hit the walls of the buildings around, sounding clearly to other people in the street, and catching Archie on the face and head. The boy had started to walk towards the distillery at the time, and was only around thirty yards from MacLaurin's window. Bloodied, shocked and in pain, he went to John MacCorquodale, a colleague of his dad's who was standing close by, and said "Damn him, he's shot me!". MacCorquodale later testified that there hadn't been any crowds of youths molesting MacLaurin's window that day, but of course he would be biased.[27]

MacCorquodale and the others took young Archie home, besmeared with blood as he was, where his father put him to bed and called a doctor. Dr. John Peter McGregor arrived that evening at the Munn's house (although Dr. MacGregor says they brought Archie to him), where he found the boy with "trifling injuries" including a scratch on the skin near his right eye but no blood, and a puncture at the corner of the right brow with some blood. He couldn't tell whether these injuries were caused by a shot but he did find some very small grains of lead in Archie's forehead. The injuries however weren't life threatening, and since the boy was still in pain, Dr. MacGregor applied a cold poultice. Eight or nine days later, after a visit by his friend John Campbell, Archie was still in pain with the lead shot, and it stayed in his head, presumably the remainder of his life.

It was a few weeks before Dr. MacLaurin was called up to face the authorities. He gave in a statement to the local JP and in the presence of the Fiscal, and several other worthy gentlemen, and when asked if he would apply for bail, he refused. Doing so would indicate his guilt he said, but when later committed to custody, and perhaps faced with his fellow prisoners (a murderous fisherman included [28]) and the (admittedly rather luxurious compared to the old place) conditions at the Inveraray jail, he changed his mind, and was released on bail. It took another three months before the summons for witnesses went out, with all except one receiving the message personally, and all turning up at court on the requested day. One teenage witness refused to give a statement unless he was paid a fair sum of money, but he later did so, although it isn't specified whether he got his fee or not.

The trial for the (dubiously!) venerable Dr. Malcolm MacLaurin was a Circuit Court one, such as murderers faced and the charge a serious one, that of violently, wickedly and felonously discharging a loaded gun towards someone in the street; there must have been a fair amount of gossip going round those Oban streets, when the news got out that such an unpopular medic (among the lowborn Òbanaich anyway) was due to stand in the dock. It was a full five months after the incident, but in the end, with no record of any sentence, one can only assume that this was another case which was dismissed, perhaps on Dr. MacGregor's evidence. [29]

Whether Malcolm MacLaurin was popular or not, he didn't live five years after his court appearance. One morning in June 1834, he'd just got up, got dressed and was reaching out for his watch, when he collapsed, dead on his bedroom floor, perhaps in the presence of a relative or servant, otherwise who would have known about the circumstances? He was buried close to his family out at Ardchattan, leaving behind an illegitimate son, who also appears to have lived in the town when he wasn't serving as a Captain in the Navy. [30]

Young John Campbell, the minister's son, presumably

continued to live with his parents and sisters on Tweedale street until he was older. He may have been the one living in Stafford street at the time of the first census, but with such a common name, he's untraceable in later years.[31]

As for Archie Munn, he seems to be the one who married a local girl and had at least one son and two grandsons. He died in Oban in 1887 and was buried near his family at the old Kilbride burial ground south of town. He seems to have had a brother and there were Munns buried in the modern cemetery north of Oban in later years.[32] Their legacy to the town includes an award-winning funeral directors, while the immediate vicinity of Dr. MacLaurin's house stayed in approximately the same genre of professionals for decades, with a pharmacy next door for many years.[33]

It seems that the other medics who served the people of Oban over the years since Malcolm MacLaurin, were popular, professional and not inclined to use a fouling gun against human or sparrow; one of them even had a hospital named after him.[34] Modern medics still stick together in difficult circumstances, and for the west coast towns, island or mainland, it's to be hoped that their impact on history is equally as good – or at least better than the notorious Malcolm MacLaurin's.

FOOTNOTES

1. "A History of Scotland" by J.D. Mackie, published Penguin Books Ltd, Middlesex, 1964, pp.324,330; "Encyclopaedia of Scotland " by John Keay and Julia Keay published Harper Collins, London 1994, p.945.
2. "Encyclopaedia of Scotland " by John Keay and Julia Keay published Harper Collins, London 1994, p.869.

3. SC54/10/14, available in the National Records of Scotland historic search room, Edinburgh; Chisholm's death certificate, will, marriage and the baptisms of his children available on scotlandpeople.com

4. Death certificate and will available on scotlandspeople.com

5. SC54/10/14, available in the National Records of Scotland historic search room, Edinburgh.

6. The Royal Commission on the Ancient and Historical Monuments of Scotland volume 3, Mull, Tiree, Coll & Northern Argyll, published Edinburgh 1980, pp.235-236.

7. SC54/10/14, available in the National Records of Scotland historic search room, Edinburgh.

8. Ibid.

9. "Encyclopaedia of Scotland " by John Keay and Julia Keay published HarperCollins, London 1994, p.661; "History of the MacKenzies" by Alexander MacKenzie, text available online.

10. Ibid.

11. SC54/10/14, available in the National Records of Scotland historic search room, Edinburgh.

12. CS44/128/40, available in the National Records of Scotland historic search room, Edinburgh.

13. Wills and death certificates available on scotlandspeople.com

14. "Encyclopaedia of Scotland " by John Keay and Julia Keay published HarperCollins, London 1994, p.661; "History of the MacKenzies" by Alexander MacKenzie, text available online.

15. Will and death certificate available on scotlandspeople.com

16. Ibid.

17. https://www.aniodhlann.org.uk/wp.content/ uploads/2019.44.1.pdf

18. Ibid.

19. The location of MacLaurin's house is specified by a few witnesses (JC26/1829/56; AD14/29/303) by which means it is possible, with local knowledge, to pinpoint the place as being this particular property.

20. JC26/1829/56; AD14/29/303 in the National Records of Scotland historic search room, Edinburgh.

21. Testimony of Nicky Sweeney, Angler's Corner, Oban, to whom the author is indebted; also www.rampfesthudson.com

22. JC26/1829/56; AD14/29/303 in the National Records of Scotland historic search room, Edinburgh.

23. AD14/29/303 in the National Records of Scotland historic search room, Edinburgh, in which young John is stated to be the son of Rev. John Campbell, minister in Oban; the only one of such

a name and profession at that time was the Congregational minister.

24. Testimony of K.Lindsay, Oban Beer Seller, to whom the author is indebted, and the author's site visit there, 2022.

25. JC26/1829/56; AD14/29/303 in the National Records of Scotland historic search room, Edinburgh.

26. Testimony of Nicky Sweeney, Angler's Corner, Oban, to whom the author is indebted; also www.rampfesthudson.com

27. JC26/1829/56; AD14/29/303 in the National Records of Scotland historic search room, Edinburgh.

28. HH21/35/1; JC26/1829/145, National Records of Scotland historic search room, Edinburgh.

29. JC26/1829/56; AD14/29/303 in the National Records of Scotland historic search room, Edinburgh.

30. https://www.aniodhlann.org.uk/wp.content/uploads/2019.44.1.pdf

31. Census 1841, available on scotlandspeople.com, when Rev. Campbell was living with his wife and other children on Tweedale street, later being buried in the Old Parish Kirk burial ground; there is a John Campbell of approximate age also living at the time in Stafford street.

32. Monumental Inscriptions, Kilbride burial ground, where there is also a stone erected by A&M Munn for their father who died in 1838. Also Monumental Inscriptions Pennyfuir burial ground, 1935.

33. Several local sources including eg. "Old Oban" by Michael Hopkin, published Stenlake Publishing, Ayrshire, 2000, p.12.

34. The former MacKelvie hospital was named after Dr. Robert Barbour MacKelvie.

•

THREE

In the churning civic unrest which accompanied the Reform riots of the early decades of the 19ᵗʰ century (and which had made the court at Inveraray so edgy at the time of the 1820 Kilchrenan riot), criminality of course rocketed. That criminality was still churning by 1828, and of course included a criminal underworld. Hidden deep within that criminal underworld was 'The Yellow Trade' ie. the making of forged coins, bank notes and bogus documentation of all types. Common throughout this era, the industry was organised and worked by skilled artisans, who crafted the fake coins from various melted or cut out metals and alloys, stamped, pressed, and finished so as to be convincing. Once the fake coins were made, they passed initially to wholesalers, who in turn passed them onto the 'smashers' who put them into general circulation, the industry being paid for by the real coins received by the smashers in their change, especially in circumstances where the smasher could confuse the retailer during the transaction.[1]

There were coiners and forgers working in Glasgow in the 1820s,[2] risking arrest and the severest of punishments for the capital crime it was. From Glasgow, these fakes would have been deliberately spread to the suburbs and rural counties such as Argyll[3], probably assuming the authorities there wouldn't be as alert as their city counterparts, nor as determined in their quest for the illegal coinage and the pedlars of such.

One of these pedlars, Mary Malcolm, arrived in Argyll in January 1828 from Glasgow, she said to stay with her daughter and son-in-law. In the following few weeks, Mary travelled a fair way over the Lochgilphead and Craignish areas, buying and selling goods and distributing fake coins, with a swift back-track to Glasgow in the middle of it all. Quite what she received from her Glasgow contact on that visit isn't stated, but she later did the Lochgilphead round again with more fake coins.

She didn't have long to practise her trade however and the authorities soon came knocking at the door of the lodging house where she and her family were staying; the coins and other goods in her possession left her with a three month sentence at Inveraray, the only curiosity being some grey and white powder discovered in a coat pocket, the truth of which may turn out in a later case.

If Mary Malcolm had been about her nefarious work in the Lochgilphead district, this was nothing against the work of another couple of pedlars who arrived in Argyll shortly afterwards. Perhaps the Glasgow supplier decided to appoint someone else as his Argyll distributor, but whatever the reason, he didn't count on another piece in the armoury of the Argyll courts. The name of this piece of armoury was Paddy MacDonald, and he was the parish constable at Lochgilphead.[9]

In the days before an organised police force such as Glasgow had, Argyll, along with other rural counties in 19th century Britain, used parish constables as their on-the-ground means of enforcing law and order. These men were appointed ideally by the parish, but in Scotland at least, by any laird influential and public-minded enough to pay their wages. Even after the advent of the police in Argyll, some parish constables still served the smaller towns, and were issued with batons, and 'cuffs' like the police constables. Derided at the time as bumbling, incapable old men in long coats, they were infact highly effective, and successful, if solitary, members of the community, working hard in increasingly difficult conditions. They were often former military men, young enough to be active in seeking out and apprehending criminals, mature enough to have the confidence in such a role, but perhaps not middle-class enough to join the Excise, the other career prospect for a former serviceman. As locals with no higher status than their criminal counterparts however, the parish constables weren't usually viewed with the respect they deserved.[10]

The parish constable in Lochgilphead doesn't appear to have been working at the time of Mary Malcolm's sojourn in the town, [11] and the appointment of one may have been inspired by the episode. This (apparently first) constable appears to have been English born, as were his younger children, but he may have had strong Irish connections, and his wife appears to have been Irish. [12] He was certainly working in Lochgilphead in December 1828, when he and his wife had their baby boy (they already had two children) baptised,[13] and by spring the following year, Paddy MacDonald had some adversaries.

These two adversaries arrived in Argyll at the end of April 1829. One of them, Mary Hamilton, had left Glasgow a few weeks before, and with Dumbarton woman Mary Hannay had gone to Greenock to take the steam ferry to Dunoon. Like Mary Malcolm before them, the women were both Irish, both middle-aged, and both apparently well-used to travelling the country as hawkers, leaving their husbands back home. Arriving at the quay at Greenock, they found a large parcel, presumably abandoned, wrapped outwardly in woollen blanketing, which being opportunists, they picked up and took with them. When they later opened the parcel, they found it contained coins, which the women kept. After all, what else could one do with such a parcel, especially since they were now outwith the jurisdiction of any of Greenock's finest parish constabulary?[14]

After disembarking from the ferry at Dunoon, the two women immediately made their way to Inveraray, where they stayed the first night at Mrs. Balfour's lodging house in Main street. They paid their landlady with good money and left a parcel, tied up with woollen blanketing, which they said would be collected by a Mrs. Stewart, who would take it to Dumbarton.

Their first task, as with any woman staying away from home, was to do some shopping, so they called at the grocery shop in Inveraray owned by the indefatigable Ann Gardner. Ann was a long-term shopkeeper in the town, and not unfamiliar with the courts, having reported her abusive husband some years before, and complained about bad service from a supplier on another occasion. [15] She certainly didn't seem to be the sort to be fooled by fake coins, and at first didn't seem to be falling for the pair's tricks. They'd asked

Ann if she wanted to buy anything from them, although according to Ann, they didn't seem to have anything to sell, a curious scenario which may reflect on their later behaviour. Infact they called back at her shop two or three times that day; perhaps they were hoping to meet her husband and 'sell' him something! Eventually, presumably without meeting Ann's drunken, abusive husband on the way, they bought some tea, sugar and tobacco, offering what later turned out to be a fake shilling in payment. They didn't have enough copper coins to pay for the goods they said, and eventually, after what may have been some wheeler dealing on the women's part, attempting a classic coiner's trick of bamboozling the shop keeper with various transactions to gain good money and leave some bad money in the shopkeepers till, Ann Gardner was left with three shillings. She had a habit of waiting until she got a pound's worth of coins, then changing them somewhere, somehow for a bank note, which on this occasion she tried to do with the help of a local vintner. The vintner's wife though, after having the shillings rejected by a customer, told Ann that the coins were fake, and Ann gave her back the bank note.[176]At this point of course, poor Ann Gardner, out of pocket by three shillings and some goods, had no idea what was about to happen elsewhere in the district.

It was a Sunday when Mary Hannay and Mary Hamilton arrived at Auchindrain, complete with a basket of eggs to sell. They may have met one Archie Campbell who lived just beyond the village,[17] somewhere else that morning, as he was "strolling"'outside his cottage when they arrived, a strangely leisurely occupation for a farm worker in spring, so he and the women may have come to a prior arrangement.

Archie's wife Nan was spinning, probably in the doorway of the cottage, at the time, so it may have been difficult for the women and Archie to enact any such arrangement at that point, if indeed they'd done so. The maidservant was also around.

On seeing Nan spinning in the cottage, the two Marys tried to sell her some eggs, but Nan didn't want to buy any. The women then tried buying some yarn from her, and eventually she sold them some of the stuff she was spinning, perhaps reckoning she'd be better off with the straight cost of such items, than spinning them up for other use. Unfortunately it was a bad decision, as they paid Nan with what she and the maid thought was a bad shilling, which she showed her husband when he came in. He thought it was a genuine coin, and besides, they'd flirted with him as they left (again, perhaps hinting at the other 'services' which they were offering to sell!), so he made a joke of it all. It was only later on when Nan Campbell tried to spend the coin herself, that she found it was indeed fake.[18]

At this stage it has to be commented on as to the way that all the female shopkeepers, in line with the practises of society at the time, defer to the men, even to a teenage boy, when judging whether the coins are genuine or not. Even though half the time the men thought the coins were real, curiously, in many such cases, the women's suspicions are correct, even if they only became doubtful after the two Marys had left the scene. There was of course a distinct difference in the weight of the coins, and the classic trick of biting one or hitting it on the floor to test the genuineness, dates from this time. The fakes, because of the lead content, were softer, heavier and easily took a tooth-mark or a dent. [19]

Back at Auchindrain, and having off-loaded some fake coins to Nan Campbell, and picked up some skeins of wool, the two Marys continued along Loch Fyneside to a place on the parish boundary, on the banks of the Leacann Water.

It was on the Monday, probably in the afternoon, when the two Marys called off at the house of John Munro at the sawmill, to make some purchases. John's wife clearly ran some sort of grocery shop there, although John himself was away from home at the time. Mrs. Munro's two customers that afternoon however didn't have enough coppers on them, so one of the two women gave her a half crown piece for the sugar and tea; Mrs Munro gave the women some change of two shillings and tuppence. She'd been doubtful about the validity of the half crown piece she'd received and she asked the advice of one of her husband's employees, young Neil Buchanan from Inveraray. Neil thought the coin was genuine, so Mrs. Munro put it into her husband's money chest.

It was the following day before the two Marys pitched up at Lochgilphead, going straight to Mrs. Sinclair's lodging house in the village. Like when they'd arrived at Inveraray, their first task on the Tuesday morning was to go shopping; no guesses as to how they intended to pay for that shopping!

One of the establishments the two women called at was managed by Margaret MacPhail, and the women bought two ounces of salt from her, paying for it with a shilling. Margaret, again suspicious about the validity of the coin, took it to show her neighbour, who said it looked fake, so she returned it to her waiting customers, who gave her back the salt.

The women's next stop was Mary Paton's shop, where they tried to buy some pork for five pence, which they again offered a shilling for. Mrs. Paton accepted the shilling, pocketing it, and gave them the change. Rather later when a neighbour called round asking for a loan of two shillings, she gave the money to her, including the fake coin. It was only then that Mary Paton realised that the coin wasn't genuine.

Before then though, the two women 'smashers' had also called at Henny MacTavish's where they'd bought half a gill of whisky with a half crown piece. Unfortunately, Henny didn't have enough money to pay the women the change, so the latter offered them a shilling to pay for the whisky instead. Again, the shopkeeper doubted the genuineness of this shilling, and showed it to a neighbour, who advised that it seemed odd, so she took it back to the two Marys and they swapped it for a real one.

Perhaps after being challenged by a few people in Lochgilphead, the two women didn't want to push their luck, so it was Wednesday before they tried shopping with the fake money again. This time, it was Chirsty MacLachlan, another vintner's wife whom they targetted, trying to buy some beef from her, but failing. So they settled for another gill of whisky instead, trying to pay for it with a half crown piece, which again, Chirsty couldn't offer the change for, so the women offered her one of the fake shillings. It seems that Chirsty wasn't as astute as her colleagues, and she accepted the dud coin.

Quite how the two Marys spent the Thursday and Friday during their stay in the Lochgilphead area isn't clear but it must have been then or at the weekend that they moved away from the village. Perhaps they realised that someone would soon become wise to their crimes, and indeed word was getting round. It got round infact to constable Paddy MacDonald.

Paddy's work was lengthy and onerous, but he set about it with care, visiting each of the shops in Lochgilphead who'd received the fake coins, talking to the shopkeepers, taking details, inspecting the coins, marking and labelling them, before visiting the lodging house where the women had stayed. Paddy must have had access to a good pony, since, with information that the women had been seen at Ardrishaig, he set off in pursuit. By the time he got there, the two Marys had left for West Otter Ferry, perhaps by boat, otherwise Paddy would have seen them en route. Off Constable MacDonald went to Otter Ferry, only to find that the women had beaten him to it, and made off towards Kilmichael, [20]probably via the many old tracks crossing the land between Port Ann and Kilmory. [21] Paddy MacDonald probably followed them over the hill, talking to the women's customers on the way, but by the time he got to Kilmichael, he found he'd been foiled again; the two Marys had done their job and left before he got there, this time heading back down the road to Cairnbaan, probably taking the route of the modern road.

Yet again, when Paddy arrived at Cairnbaan, he found he'd just missed them, as they'd gone along the North bank of the canal, towards the Crinan Basin. It's at this point that he probably had mixed feelings. If the women crossed over at the wee ferry for Bellanoch, and followed the canal back towards Cairnbaan along the south bank, Paddy would see them at some point, and with the help of any passing boats or lock keepers, be able to get over to them pretty quickly. Unfortunately, if the women knew the area as well as they seemed to, they would also know that a route existed from at least two points on the south bank of the canal, which could lead them up into the hills of South Knapdale and another network of tracks, cottages and farmsteads, where Paddy may well lose them. Nevertheless, Constable MacDonald began his chase again, following his quarries along the north bank of the Crinan Canal towards the Crinan Basin at the end.

It's now that the chase must have become rather exciting to watch. After receiving information that the two women were at Sarah Graham's house at Bellanoch, Paddy went over there, perhaps via the bridge which with his pony would have been easier, if indeed the bridge existed at the time. Certainly a swing bridge had existed down at Cairnbaan for many years by then, [23] but even if Paddy had requisitioned someone's boat to carry him over to Bellanoch, before he could reach the place, and perhaps realising, or even seeing Paddy coming after them, the two Marys doubled back to the north bank. Finding he'd just missed his quarries yet again, one wonders if Paddy went back over the water by the same requisitioned boat, to cut the women off, perhaps with a few locals getting involved, shouting and pointing them out?

Eventually, it was at Dougie MacLachlan's changehouse over the loch from Bellanoch that Paddy MacDonald's luck changed. He caught up with the two women, (perhaps someone had detained them for him on this occasion) and one can only imagine the scene as he apprehended them within the confines of the inn. The story probably went round the parish for months afterwards.

From the shores of the Crinan Canal, the intrepid Constable MacDonald took the two Marys back to

Lochgilphead, to his own house, where his wife must have been getting rather worried by then. Securely held there for the night, it was perhaps on the Sunday morning that he took the pair off to the house of a local JP, Dr. James (or John) Hunter, just outside the village, towards Ardrishaig. [24]

Dr. Hunter must have been quite a figure in the Lochgilphead area. In his late 30s by then, he'd married into one of the local landowners' families, and with his wife had a family of five children, including a toddler and a baby. [25] A typical doctor however, his handwriting in a later case was appalling, [26] but he was called upon to testify and serve the district in so many ways over the years, that his name pops up whenever anything official is happening.

It was at James Hunter's house that the packs and pockets of the two Marys were eventually emptied. Mary Hamilton had on her 123 fake shillings and five fake half crown pieces, some forged bank notes and a cloth, used to 'weather' the coins to make them look genuine. Mary Hannay had four shillings in fake coins, and some genuine money which was returned to her. All the fake coins and bank notes were counted, their dates and numbers made note of, they were fixed together, labelled and then wrapped up in a parcel and left with Dr. Hunter. Also with the two Marys when they were apprehended were two small parcels, one containing a white powder, the other a grey powder. [27] Some samples were taken from these and kept separate, but there isn't any comment in the trial notes of what this powder was. It might be assumed it was something which the women rubbed on the coins to make them appear genuine, but there isn't any indication of such powders being used on fake coins, although they were of course altered slightly to make them look real. It's also curious that Mary Malcolm before them had had some greyish white powder in a coat pocket when she was apprehended. Instead of being part of some trick for making counterfeit coins appear genuine, could the powder have been arsenic, classically a greyish white crystalline powder, and taken as a recreational drug by all and sundry in those days, despite the dangers? It wasn't at that time illegal, neither in the sale and purchase of it, [28] nor the use of it, but one couldn't imagine anyone willingly approving of a family member's liberal use of it, especially in an era when every penny mattered to a young family trying to make ends meet. Had Archie Campbell, a farm worker coincidentally and unusually strolling in front of his cottage that spring day at Auchindrain, been hoping to buy some arsenic from the women when they called by, or had it been something else he'd hoped to 'purchase' from them? After being apprehended, Mary Hamilton had refused to give up her husband's first name and address as she feared it would "bring shame on his family". If the greyish white powder had been arsenic, and since it wasn't illegal, could the women's other suspicious behaviour have been the root of her not wanting to bring shame on her husband's family?

Whatever the women's secret side-line during their perambulations in the Lochgilphead area, they and Paddy were still at Dr. Hunter's house well over an hour later when a couple of familiar figures arrived. Paddy's wife, accompanied by a local plasterer and their own maid servant, turned up with a small parcel. Cathie MacDonald told Dr. Hunter and her husband how after Paddy had left with the women, their maid servant had been sweeping the kitchen fireplace, just by where the women had spent the night, and in among the cinders, she found a partially burnt package. Suspecting that this was part of the haul which should have been submitted to her husband, Cathie set off with it to Dr. Hunter's, only to find herself, the maid and their escort not the only ones heading towards Ardrishaig. Chirsty MacLachlan from Lochgilphead had evidently realised the identity of the coin the women had given her in payment, and she was also on her way to show Paddy and Dr. Hunter; all these items were duly marked, labelled, wrapped up in parcels and sealed, along with the haul which Paddy had already retrieved from the two women.

The following day, with the two Marys still in custody somewhere (it's not clear where), a meeting was held at Mrs. Cranmer's pub in Lochgilphead, to enable all the local magistrates to gather together, discuss it all (suitably lubricated by Mrs. Cranmer's offerings, one can assume!) put the paperwork in order, take some statements and prepare everything for the next stage in the case, namely the involvement of the great and good at Inveraray.

Constable MacDonald was still working hard, tracking down further instances to lay before the Inveraray court, so he left his assistant to see that the two Marys were ferried, quite literally, over to the neighbouring town. While the women and Paddy's assistant were standing on the pier at Lochgilphead waiting for the steamer to collect them, Mary Hannay asked the young man to write a letter for her to her son, requesting that some clothes be sent to her. The other Mary also asked for a message to be included in the letter; that her husband should pick up some money owed to her at Dumbarton, then come to Inveraray to see her in jail, enquiring for her by the name 'Mrs. Campbell'.

The strange circumstance of someone collecting money to deliver to a fake coin pedlar was enough to spark the young man's suspicions, and he asked where Mary's husband lived, but she wouldn't tell him. All she would say was that the addressee knew where her husband lived, and the letter was duly addressed to one George Stewart in Dumbarton, and off the two Marys went, with Paddy's assistant, to Inveraray, where the women were detained until their trial.

The following day on the border of the parish with Inveraray, the sawmill worker John Munro, whose wife had encountered the two women the previous week had a visitor one evening, just before dark. John's neighbour Mrs. Kirk, the wife of his manager, came seeking some coins to exchange for a bank note she had. Evidently eager to help a neighbour, John dipped into his money chest and retrieved enough coins to swap for the bank note, and away Mrs. Kirk went. Shortly afterwards, John Munro had another visitor, this time the parish constable from Lochgilphead, explaining how numbers of counterfeit money had been passed around the parish. This seemed to jog John Munro's memory and he must have had a sudden realisation – he'd just passed a fake coin to Mrs. Kirk! He and his wife sent their son Donald off to the Kirks' house to swap the bank note back for the coins, including the fake one, and the lad fulfilled the errand correctly, the fake being handed over to Paddy MacDonald for marking, labelling and parcelling up.

The weeks and months passed for the women, holed up in the new jail on Crown Point (both denying passing fake coins to anyone), and as usual the Inveraray court business passed as ponderously as it always did. Come the time of the autumn visit of the Circuit Court, Lord Justice Clark and his court staff stayed in the town, and among their subjects that day, was the trial of Mary Hamilton and Mary Hannay. As expected, various witnesses were called up, chiefly those who could testify that the coins which Paddy MacDonald had marked and sealed were actually the self same coins which they were being shown in court. The bundle which the two Marys had left with Mrs. Balfour was opened up for the first time aswell, and found to contain nothing more criminal than two pairs of blankets and a pair of cord breeches, the which were returned to the prisoners.

The chief witness of course was Paddy MacDonald himself, and his testimony proves that he wasn't just an intrepid, determined character, but he clearly had an acute, financial mind along with it; he testified with due clarity to the numerous parcels, coins and bank notes, described how he'd gathered them all, the exact days and dates, the names of the witnesses, place names and circumstances, exact figures and amounts of money; so many small, but crucial, facts, figures and witnesses that at one point an index had to be made. Not even the court clerk could keep a tab on all the details, although Paddy MacDonald largely could.

All this vast amount of detail, facts and figures meant more work than normal for the court, but of course it didn't make any difference to the conviction for Mary Hamilton and Mary Hannay; they were both found guilty and sentenced to nine more months behind bars at Inveraray. Their good money (£2/12/6d) was returned to them on their release (it seems as though the debt owed to one of them at Dumbarton didn't reach her after all), and they probably used this to get out of Argyll for good.[29]

The case of the two Marys peddling fake coins, bank notes and probably arsenic and certain other 'personal services' around Lochgilphead and Inveraray was of course not the end of fake coins and coiners in Argyll. Another pair of embezzlers, this time from Campbeltown, were tried in Edinburgh just a few days afterwards, but were ultimately found not guilty,[30] while another criminal in Oban tried forging bank notes, an equally common ploy at the time.[31] It seems however that with Paddy MacDonald on the case, nothing really hit home in his part of Argyll at least. What happened to him in later years is somewhat of a mystery. The only man of his age and with an identical set of children, along with a wife of the same name, was living in Edinburgh by the time of the 1841 census, his occupation then sadly indecipherable on the original document, [32] although he doesn't seem to have died in the city. One can't imagine such a character so dedicated to law and order and serving his community, not trying to get into a police uniform of sorts if it was at all possible, so it's to be hoped that he perhaps moved his family south or over to Glasgow and joined one of the newly emerging police forces somewhere. If his own children lived to adulthood, he would certainly have had some stories to tell his grandchildren about that chase around the Crinan Canal!

FOOTNOTES

1. Victorian-Supersleuth.com; https://museum.wales/articles/1722/Counterfeit-Coins
2. Several references to forgers and dealers in counterfeit coinage working in Glasgow and the surrounding districts in the early 19th century including AD14/29/387, JC26/1828/254,

JC26/1830/249 or JC26/1830/324, available in the National Records of Scotland historic search room, Edinburgh.

3. Victorian-Supersleuth.com
4. Several sources eg."Encyclopaedia of Scotland " by John Keay and Julia Keay published Harper Collins, London 1994, p.452; "The First Statistical Account, volume xx, published c.1792, pp.56,149,391; "The Royal Burgh of Inveraray" by Alexander Fraser, published by The Saint Andrew Press, Edinburgh 1977, p.13 n.8.
5. JC26/1828/24, available in the National Records of Scotland historic search room, Edinburgh.
6. Ibid.
7. historyofparliamentonline.org; wikipedia.org/wiki/Sir_WilliamRae_3rd_Baronet
8. JC26/1828/24, available in the National Records of Scotland historic search room, Edinburgh.
9. AD14/29/302; JC26/1829/172; HH21/35/1, available in the National Records of Scotland historic search room, Edinburgh.
10. "The story of Crime and Punishments" (BBC History Magazine) published Immediate Media Company, Bristol Ltd, 2018, p.56; https://en.wikipedia.org/wiki/parish_constable
11. Clearly, if there'd been a parish constable in the village at the time of Mary Malcolm's misdemeanours, he'd have been mentioned in the trial notes; needless to say, there isn't any such mention.
12. The only Patrick MacDonald with a Catherine as a wife, and the same run of children, of similar ages, is living in Edinburgh at the time of the 1841 census (Grassmarket), and on this record his wife is stated as being born in Ireland, he being born in England, and his children in either Scotland, Ireland or England.
13. Baptism, Old Parish Registers, South Knapdale parish, 1828, John MacDonald, available on scotlandspeople.com
14. AD14/29/302; JC26/1829/172; HH21/35/1, available in the National Records of Scotland historic search room, Edinburgh.
15. "Inveraray Burgh Court Processes 1686-1825, Deeds, Bonds of Caution etc 1710-1810", edited by Frank Bigwood, November 1820.
16. AD14/29/302; JC26/1829/172; HH21/35/1, available in the National Records of Scotland historic search room, Edinburgh.
17. Testimony of Bob Clark and Rachael Thomas, Auchindrain Township Museum, to whom the author is indebted.
18. AD14/29/302; JC26/1829/172; HH21/35/1, available in the National Records of Scotland historic search room, Edinburgh.
19. Victorian-Supersleuth.com; museum.wales/articles/1722/

Counterfeit-Coins; cdn.lbma.org.uk/items/why-do-pirates-and-champions-bite-gold-coins-and-medals.pdf, a paper by Arnaud Manas, 2018.

20. AD14/29/302; JC26/1829/172; HH21/35/1, available in the National Records of Scotland historic search room, Edinburgh.

21. Visible on several old maps eg.Arrowsmith 1807, Langlands 1804 and the early OS maps compared with modern (Pathfinder) maps, all available on maps.nls.uk/Scotland/index.html.

22. The Crinan Canal murder, JC13/33/44v; JC26/1804/37 and 39, at the National Records of Scotland historic search room, Edinburgh.

23. Included in JC13/33/44v; JC26/1804/37 and 39, as the site of a murder. See also "Blood and Battery, murder, riot and theft in old Argyll" by Lindsay Campbell, published Troubador, Leicestershire, 2021, p.76.

24. AD14/29/302; JC26/1829/172; HH21/35/1, available in the National Records of Scotland historic search room, Edinburgh.

25. Baptisms, Old Parish Registers, South Knapdale parish, Alex 1829, James 1826 and three others, available on scotlandspeople website. Also Dr. Hunter's wife's death certificate January 1881, St.Vincent crescent, Glasgow.

26. The medical report included in a murder in Lochgilphead in 1844, JC26/1844/242.

27. AD14/29/302; JC26/1829/172; HH21/35/1, available in the National Records of Scotland historic search room, Edinburgh.

28. https://crosscut.com/2010/09/arsenic-victorians-secret.

29. AD14/29/302; JC26/1829/172; HH21/35/1, available in the National Records of Scotland historic search room, Edinburgh.

30. JC26/1829/300, available in the National Records of Scotland historic search room, Edinburgh.

31. JC26/1827/403; also a single banknote forger working in Lochgilphead before the women's time there: JC26/1827/415, available in the National Records of Scotland historic search room, Edinburgh.

32. See ref. 13.

33. Neither of these men appear to be old enough to have been Paddy (even allowing for inconsistencies due to eg.the census enumerator rounding up ages), but their deaths are recorded as happening at the Royal Infirmary, St.Cuthbert's parish, Edinburgh in October and November 1848, see scotlandspeople. com

FOUR

L ate one night in November 1881, a storm hit the Argyll coast. Not an unusual scenario at any time of year, and the coastal communities on the Slate Islands were well used to such storms. Come the following morning however, there was a change in the layout of one of these communities. One of the slate quarries on the shore, a sizeable area bearing valuable equipment, engineering works and slate stock, was completely flooded by a breach in the natural wall dividing it from the sea, effectively turning a working quarry into a lagoon.[1] This disastrous event however didn't only put a permanent stop to quarrying on that spot, it also sealed the lid on any trace of the movements of a group of men some fifty years earlier, two of whom became accused of murder.

The slate quarrying industries on the islands off the coast of Lorn had a long history, even at that time. It had been back in 1745 that the Marble and Slate Company of Nether Lorn had begun an industry which within a few decades was employing considerable quantities of locals, men working the quarry faces, others splitting the subsequent products into useable sized slates, and labourers and women and children fetching and carrying. Ships would come into the pier to collect the slates for distribution all over the world, other artisans worked alongside the quarriers, and the industry slowly but literally changed the face of the landscape, while the workers lived in specially built rows of cottages, cheek by jowl with the quarries they worked.[2] Among these quarriers, labourers and other workers associated with the island industry, the MacPhail brothers from Easdale Island, sons of the late schoolmaster, had engendered an argument with one Duncan Livingston, another quarrier living there. Early on the morning of Wednesday 12th January 1831, Duncan, with a certain amount of alcohol in him, had been in the MacPhail's cottage settling an argument. Easier said than done though, and Duncan's friends had to call him out of the place eventually, none of the men exactly parting on pleasant terms.

Later that day, and with dusk coming on quickly, and the ferry due to leave for Ellenabeich, all three men involved in the argument piled into the boat, alongside several other locals. The MacPhail brothers were heading for Dunmore to make a complaint about Livingston to their manager, Mr. Campbell.[3] Quite why Duncan Livingston was also in the boat isn't specified, but with them there, were the MacPhails' uncle and aunt, a brother-in-law, and other local men with their wives, and some children. The ferryman was a rather over-confident 16 year old, probably still an apprentice, but he seemed capable enough.

The few minutes journey over to Ellenabeich was hardly peaceful. Both the MacPhail brothers and Livingston continued the argument; the latter threatened to put out the eyes of Dugie MacPhail, while his brother said that he daren't do such a thing. Livingston then damned Neil and threatened to throw him overboard, resulting in Dugie asking two of the other men there to keep him quiet.

The pier the boat landed at isn't the current one where the visitors flock in summer, but the older one round the corner, with a sunken way of slate leading up to the village. One of the quarries, the one flooded by the storm fifty years later, sat at one side of the sunken way, but was considerably smaller than it was at the time of the flooding. Certainly there was a pathway leading from the pier past the quarry and over to another established track between the rows of cottages, which eventually led to the main road and Mr. Campbell's house.

Once the boat had pulled up at the great old wooden pier, Neil MacPhail got out first, followed by his brother and Duncan Livingston, while their Auntie Mary went to speak to one John MacQueen who was waiting on shore to meet someone else from the boat. She was glad to get off the ferry, she said, since her two nephews and Livingston had been having "high words" together on the crossing, never a safe thing to do with the Atlantic breakers around you.[5]

John MacQueen was in his forties,[6] also a quarrier by trade[7] and with a wife and young family in the village.[8] His testimony is later branded "stupid" by someone in the courts, possibly the Fiscal himself, but set in the context of the incident, he seems to have been the mature, unbiased and stabilising influence on the younger men there.[9]

With the MacPhails' auntie talking to MacQueen, and Livingston presumably talking to someone else, the brothers and their uncle stood by a garden close to the shore deep in conversation for a few minutes. Possibly their uncle was trying to calm the brothers down, or maybe they were getting their stories straight before heading off to Mr. Campbell's house.

Within a few minutes of the boat pulling into the ferry, the brothers and their uncle all turned to walk away from the shore, Duncan Livingston following them and shouting "Stand to now!" when they didn't respond. Neil MacPhail looked back and saw Livingston approaching but by the time Duncan had caught up with them, they were probably on the other side of the quarry, and certainly by the rising ground closer to the track near what is now The Engine House.[11] It was here that Livingston overtook the three men, jumping onto a garden wall, and damning Neil McPhail again from there.[12]

With little further invitation required, Neil pulled Livingston from the wall, at which the latter struck his opponent, grabbed him by the breast and they both fell, fighting and struggling onto the ground. Livingston was on top of Neil, both probably trading punches and curses, and it took Dugie MacPhail, their uncle and some others to help Neil to his feet, leaving Livingston still on the ground, still of course drunk, and still trying to grab Neil round the legs. All three MacPhails then continued the fight with the grounded man, striking him on the head and body, in one testimony only with their hands, feet and fists, in another with a blunt edged piece of slate, at least 3 or 4 times, on the side of his head. John MacQueen was trying to separate them all, and when he did eventually manage to get them apart, Neil told his brother that they might definitely make a complaint to Mr. Campbell now, and they left the scene.[13]

The slate which had been used on Livingston, around 5lb in weight,[14] would have been capable of doing some considerable damage especially in the hands of the strong, experienced men who were the slaters and quarriers holding it. One witness later said the strikes sounded not unlike the strikes a butcher used to kill an animal, and the blunt force trauma such damage effected would have cracked bone and caused swelling and bleeding below.[15]

Duncan Livingston, despite the severe blows he'd received and of course given back, managed to get to his feet after the MacPhails left, and tried to chase after them. He was only held back by John MacQueen's efforts, though the injured man was fighting so hard that he nearly throttled MacQueen, trying to escape his clutches.

In between the spot where the men had been fighting and the road leading to Dunmore (now the main road), the trackway on which the MacPhails were walking was, like the sunken way by the old pier, bounded by slate walls and referred to in the old records as a "pass". It was only a couple of minutes walk from where the fight had taken place, and MacQueen and the others, once Livingston had got away from them, had seen the latter run to the pass, jump onto the wall bounding it, then disappear from view over the other side. When they reached the place themselves, they found Livingston lying on his back, motionless but groaning.[16]

MacQueen and the other man quickly came to Livingston's side. On the streets of old Ellenabeich, there were standpipes set up for the inhabitants to help themselves to fresh water,[17] and with perhaps a handy bowl somewhere nearby, one of the men tried to get Livingston to take a drink, but his jaws appeared locked; it seems that whatever head injuries he'd sustained in the fight had left him with spasms so intense that he may have been immobile, even rigid. He may have still been conscious, but he certainly couldn't swallow anything, although there didn't seem to be any marks of violence on him. One of the men said he thought he was dead, but MacQueen managed to lift him up and get him to his house, which must have been fairly close.

As for the MacPhail brothers and their uncle, they'd meanwhile continued onto Dunmore, only to find neither Mr. Campbell nor his clerk at home. With dusk coming on fast, they decided to return to Uncle MacPhail's house, but on their way there, met John MacQueen who was heading out to fetch the doctor. MacQueen started to reprimand the younger MacPhails, but Neil gave back as good as he got. If MacQueen was going to take Livingston's part in the argument, he said, he needed to "stand to it now". Dugie MacPhail told MacQueen that his hand had erred if hadn't given Livingston what would settle the argument, even if he was punished for what he'd just done. The younger MacPhails then set off back towards their uncle's house, although they afterwards returned to the ferry and were soon home.

Darkness had set in by then, and back in Ellenabeich, Dr. Sinclair arrived at John MacQueen's house. Livingston was no better, and when the first ferry left for the island the following morning, an ominous message would have gone with it to Livingston's parents. Their son was dead; his body was returned to the island later that day and taken to his parent's house where it lay until the Friday, when the postmortem examination took place. Reviewing the results of this and in the light of modern forensic knowledge, it seems that both the fight with the MacPhails and the fall in the 'pass' were the cause of the internal injuries Livingston suffered. The kicks from Neil MacPhail when he was trying to extricate himself from Livingston's grip undoubtedly caused some severe damage, but the strikes from the slate and from the fall in the pass would also have contributed to the trauma to his skull and the bleeding on his brain. However these injuries were sustained, Dr. Sinclair's conclusion was that Livingston had died as a result of injuries sustained during the argument with the MacPhails. Duncan Livingston's body was transferred the same day, to the old burial ground on the mainland, where his headstone is still visible.[20]

In a surprisingly swift course of events, both Neil and Dugie MacPhail were at Inveraray within three days, making their statements infront of the Sheriff Substitute. Within these statements, lengthy and wordy though they are, it's almost possible to hear the MacPhails' own voices. Neil's statement particularly displays an education surely higher than normal for a working class man, which can only have come from his father's personal tutoring; words and phrases are used which are more than just the lawyer-speak of the clerk, proved by the fact that his younger brother isn't quite so articulate. Neil's signature at the bottom of every page though hints at the stress he's undergoing while making the statement; his handwriting becomes more weak and scrawly the further on he goes (he even misspells his own surname at one point), although Dugie doesn't seem to have had such an anxious time in the Sheriff's office.[21]

It was April before the MacPhail brothers' trial came up, and the summons were sent out to all the witnesses, with the exception of course of Uncle MacPhail who was too close to the accused to be called to testify. The young ferryman was called up and described the slate which had been used to strike Livingston (described it in terms normally used by a surgeon, so whether the prosecution was leading him, or it was just teenage cockiness, imitating Dr. Sinclair's terminology, is impossible to tell). Livingston's mother stands in court telling how the argument started and how she was informed of her son's death. His father however was 'indisposed' and unable to attend court, and one wonders if father, aswell as son, was prone to alcohol abuse.

Beside the list of witnesses amongst the trial paperwork, someone in the court wrote a summary of their opinion of almost every one, not always flattering, and certainly it seems unkind and inaccurate. Many of the names have "proves nothing" scribbled next to them, some (like John MacQueen) are declared "stupid" while another is noted as a "bad witness". At the end of their (supposedly ineffective) testimonies, all these "useless" witnesses returned to their homes on Easdale or at Ellenabeich while the MacPhail brothers were found guilty of culpable homicide. [23]

In the wake of such a tragic case as this, there is still one mystery remaining. Dugie McPhail was sentenced to fourteen years transportation, which should have seen him out of Britain from 1831 to 1845, if indeed he survived. In 1864 however, he died in Glasgow (ironically on the same date Duncan Livingston died, all those years before, and even more ironically of a brain disorder, not unlike Livingston). [24] Prior to that date, he'd been living in the city since at least 1841, and had fathered children who'd been born there between 1836 and 1850.[25] Moreover, his brother Neil also lived and worked in Glasgow at the same time, crucially as a slater. It truly seems as though both MacPhail brothers had escaped a transportation sentence, with no hint in the old records as to how and why. The brothers' own families followed them to Glasgow, and the men clearly stayed in touch, since Neil's widow was later buried close to Dugie, although Neil may have died elsewhere.[26]

We'll probably never know why the MacPhail brothers were relieved of their sentence, and there isn't any meaningful conclusion which can be drawn in this case. All we know is that back in Kilbrandon parish, their uncle and John MacQueen continued their parts in the Slate industry,[27] and all were eventually laid to rest in the same burial ground as Duncan Livingston,[28] where the same chill Atlantic wind blasts the slate headstones as harshly as it does the slate rooved cottages in the village and on the island. The slate industry eventually died, while that storm and flood in 1881 put the lid on any memory of the three men whose argument saw the death of one of them among the very slates they'd quarried, and with one of those very slates as the weapon that dealt the final blow.

FOOTNOTES

1. The Royal Commission on the Ancient and Historical Monuments of Scotland, Argyll volume 2, Lorn, 1974, p.279.
2. The Royal Commission on the Ancient and Historical Monuments of Scotland, Argyll volume 2, Lorn, 1974, p.278-279; "The First Statistical Account", volume xx, published c.1792, pp.173-175; "The Second Statistical Account" volume 7, Renfrew-Argyll, published by Blackwood and Sons, Edinburgh 1845, pp.77-78, 79.
3. JC26/1831/94; AD14/31/198, available in the National Records of

Scotland historic search room, Edinburgh.

4. Dugald MacPhail's statement, JC26/1831/94 available in the National Records of Scotland historic search room, Edinburgh.

5. Various old maps eg.Arrowsmiths 1807, Langlands 1804 and the early OS maps all available on maps.nls.uk/Scotland/index.html.

6. Census Return 1841, Kilbrandon parish, available on scotlandspeople.com

8. Ibid.

9. JC26/1831/94; AD14/31/198, available in the National Records of Scotland historic search room, Edinburgh.

10. Ibid.

11. JC26/1831/94; AD14/31/198, available in the National Records of Scotland historic search room, Edinburgh; the author's site visit, April 2022, to trace the approximate route the men took from the old pier.

12. JC26/1831/94; AD14/31/198, available in the National Records of Scotland historic search room, Edinburgh.

13. Ibid.

14. The author's calculations based on the estimated size of the slate as in the witness statement of Dugald MacPherson (JC26/1831/94; AD14/31/198), and comparison with similar slates readily available and the testimony of the volunteers and displays at the Scottish Slate Islands Museum, Ellenabeich, to whom the author is indebted.

15. JC26/1831/94; AD14/31/198, available in the National Records of Scotland historic search room, Edinburgh; Encyclopaedia Britannica Macropaedia vol.12, pp.1054-1056; "Written in Bone, hidden stories of what we leave behind", by Sue Black, published Penguin, 2020, pp.38,47; "Forensic investigation of cranial injuries due to blunt force trauma: current best practise" by Elena F.Kranioti, 2015, available online; research.net/publication/261882041_Blunt_force_trauma_to_skull_with_various_instruments, published med.ncbi.nlm.nih.gov/3494325/

16. JC26/1831/94; AD14/31/198, available in the National Records of Scotland historic search room, Edinburgh; head injuries of course don't always kill or debilitate on the spot, the victim's fate depending on what brain damage is done, or what bleeding, if any, is happening inside the skull (Encyclopaedia Britannica Macropaedia vol.12, pp.1054-1056), sometimes creating a tetanic spasm, which can result in rigidity in the jaws, limbs etc . See also footnote 20 (below).

17. "The Easdale Doctor" by Mary Withall, published Birlinn, Edinburgh, 2018, p.47.

18. "The First Statistical Account", volume xx, published c.1792, pp.177; The Royal Commission on the Ancient and Historical Monuments of Scotland, Argyll volume 2, Lorn, 1974, p.139-140; JC26/1831/94; AD14/31/198, available in the National Records of Scotland historic search room, Edinburgh.

19. JC26/1831/94; AD14/31/198, available in the National Records of Scotland historic search room, Edinburgh.

20. Monumental Inscription at Kilbrandon burial ground, available in Argyll & Bute County archives ("Live Argyll"), Manse Brae, Lochgilphead and the author's own collection of the same; JC26/1831/94; AD14/31/198, available in the National Records of Scotland historic search room, Edinburgh; "Written in Bone, hidden stories of what we leave behind", by Sue Black, published Penguin, 2020, pp.38,47; "Forensic investigation of cranial injuries due to blunt force trauma: current best practise" by Elena F.Kranioti, 2015, available online; research.net/publication/261882041_Blunt_force_trauma_to_skull_with_various_instruments, published med.ncbi.nlm.nih.gov/3494325/

21. JC26/1831/94; AD14/31/198, available in the National Records of Scotland historic search room, Edinburgh.

22. Census returns, 1841 and 1851, (see note 25 below) and baptisms, Kilbrandon parish, 1830, available scotlandspeople.com.

23. JC26/1831/94; AD14/31/198, available in the National Records of Scotland historic search room, Edinburgh.

24. Death certificate, January 1864, Crown st, Glasgow, 57yrs, buried Southern Necropolis, Glasgow, available on scotlandspeople.com

25. 1851 census return, Thistle street, Gorbals, for Dugald and 1841 and '51 (see below) for Neil, available on scotlandspeople.com, and the ages of their various children.

26. Census returns, 1841 and 1851, South Pettigrew street, Lanark and Duke street, Glasgow, respectively; Neil's wife was a widow by 1851 cf. Census Return. In addition, there isn't any trace of an appeal by the brothers in the appropriate documents in the National Records of Scotland, Edinburgh (JC29/4,1826-1837; JC29/2, 1822-1864).

27. Census Returns 1841 and '51, Kilbrandon parish, available on scotlandspeople.com

28. Monumental Inscription at Kilbrandon burial ground, available in Argyll & Bute County archives ("Live Argyll"), Manse Brae, Lochgilphead and the author's own collection of the same.

FIVE

The peninsula of Kintyre on the west coast of Argyll has long been renowned among visitors and surfers for its golden sands and peaceful beaches. Some of those golden sands lie in a parchment coloured sickle at the very southernmost tip of Kintyre in the parish of Southend, although they may not always have been so sandy, since it's acknowledged locally that quantities of gravel were removed from the beach in recent decades.

Nevertheless, Southend is still a peaceful community, a world away from the bustle of Campbeltown only a few miles up the road, a place where you naturally want to drive slower and where people stop to talk to their neighbours in the middle of the road. The other side of that road however is a vast, steel grey roaring ocean, the beach and the ocean surely playing a part in anyone's lives there over the years and centuries.

It was in a field adjacent to that roaring ocean in 1836, that a sporting event drew the locals from near and far. There was clearly a healthy interest in the old game of shinty in Southend at the time. These matches of old, as vigorous and potentially violent as their modern counterpart, were classically played on the old festival days and on any big enough area of flat open ground between two parishes or land holdings, especially on a sea-strand or machair. There were sometimes hundreds of players, with bitter fights and local grievances settled, "the sharp crack of contact" and "the uproarious melee" often resulting in serious injury in the days before set rules and safety gear made the game no less enjoyable, if safer.[1]

At Southend in the dark days of winter 1836, Old New Years Day was coming round, and it may have been traditional to have a shinty match by the beach at Carskey Bay: whether or no, teams would have been arranged, the news would have gone round the parish like wildfire and come the day, the men congregated on the wide open flat fields between Gartvaigh and Lepenstrath.

With the game soon in full swing and locals coming from 'all airts' to watch, at some stage someone may have hit the ball rather waywardly so that it flew over onto the beach, perhaps almost disappearing there under its own weight.[3] The barge of men which subsequently charged off the field after the ball wouldn't have made finding it any easier amongst the sand and gravel, and undoubtedly tempers began to be frayed, shinty sticks raised in anger, and at some stage someone started a proper fisticuffs fight. At this point it seems the game was abandoned and all were concentrating on the fight. More locals were coming to watch, including those from Gartvain, the wee double cottage in its own hollow just off the track from Druma Voulin, among them John MacCoag, one of the tenants there, and his sister Rose.[4]

John and Rose had had a glass of whisky at Gartvain before they left, then walked down the road to the match. It was nearly 3pm by then and John picked up a discarded shinty stick by the roadside as he went, a heavy old smallish piece, which John kept hold of as they walked.[5]

By the time John and Rose got to the shinty field, or rather the beach, the fight was in full swing. A number of men were struggling with each other, flinging fists and sticks around, some angry, some fighting, some trying to calm the situation. Included in them was a big Irishman who declared that he would fight any "Scotch or Highland bugger who stood on the strand", and before long some sort of formal boxing ring had been made, which efforts John MacCoag, still largely sober, joined in with, pushing people aside, trying to prevent more fights happening amidst the main fight, and still with the shinty stick in his hand. The proponents in the main 'ring' were stripped to the waist, boxing fiercely and covered in blood. It wasn't long before any efforts at preventing the main fighting from merging with other side-fights began to fail, and the whole scene degenerated into one mass 'battle'. Shinty sticks were raised in defence and attack, local arguments were coming to the fore, and there was blood and shouting and confusion. At one point, Rose MacCoag thought she saw her brother involved in one side-fight, and called out to him, at which someone cursed her and hit her on the back of her head with a stick. She fell down, stunned, and was unconscious for some time, she had no idea how long.[6]

In the meantime, John MacCoag had indeed been involved in a side-fight, but not the one Rose saw. In the process of trying to move people away from the main fight, John had got into an argument with one Duncan MacDougall from Bailevianan. Duncan had fathered a baby girl with John's sister-in-law, but had refused to acknowledge his paternity, and the argument had been going back and forth between the two families for three years by then. For some reason, during the general melee, MacDougall had said something provoking to John MacCoag and the latter, with Donnie McIlvery, had picked up on it and raised their sticks to him. MacDougall fought the two of them back, one hand bearing the stick (the Kintyre men had a speciality for using a shinty stick one-handed[7]) the other hand fending off all comers. John was struck several times on the head and fell down at least twice. Another man helped him up, and wiped the blood and sand off his face. MacIlvery, who'd been fighting alongside John, also got hit with someone's stick, being more badly bloodied than John, but less injured and found himself able to grab hold of MacDougall and shout in his face "What's this murderous business?" he was doing.[8]

There was as much hitting and defending from John MacCoag and MacIlvery as there was from Duncan MacDougall, and another man, Duncan MacMillan from Culinlongart, and this side-fight moved back and forth, in and out of the main fight for some time. Eventually John MacCoag managed to get out of the fight, and stood alone on the beach, blood on his face and hands in his pockets, where Catherine MacKenzie, a mature woman from Keill, saw him. She asked him if he'd been fighting, and he replied "Not much" and that it was the shinty sticks which had scratched his face. Mrs. MacKenzie advised him to go home and he said he would, but he was still standing there when she went past again.

At this point in the 'battle' other men were also staggering out of the melee, bloodied and battered, and others were trying to get home, badly wounded. Rose eventually found her brother, on the beach but sitting down by that time, perhaps on the great dark rocks currently still among the sand. He didn't reply when she spoke to him, but he was sick, and he put one hand up to his head; "It's my head," he told her, then got up and made to go home. Rose went with him, but on the way up to the farm, John complained of feeling giddy, and was sick again, although he didn't have many apparent injuries and only a bit of bruising on his face.[9]

Somehow, John and Rose MacCoag managed to get up the road to John's house, with John still sick, giddy and with head pains; it isn't unusual for even severe head injury victims to be able to walk for some time afterwards, the worst damage only manifesting in later hours, after they've reached safety.[10] As for John and Rose MacCoag, when the pair reached Gartvain, John took off his coat, then went to bed fully clothed. It was only just dark by then and Mary, his wife, had spoken to him, but again, he didn't reply. Infact, John MacCoag never spoke again.

Mary and Rose stayed up a bit longer, keeping an eye on John all the time. At one point in the evening, he tried to put his head over the bedside as if he was going to be sick again, but he didn't. All he did when Rose put a hand on his forehead was groan. Some time later, she and Mary turned him in the bed, "to give him ease"; there was blood on the pillow where his left ear had been. By that time, he'd coughed up some more blood, and he had some coming from his nose, but otherwise seemed to sleep through the first part of the night. The women sat with him until 10pm, when Rose went to bed. Mary sat up for longer, eventually going to bed beside John at around midnight.[11]

Despite the events of the day, the MacCoags seemed to sleep peacefully enough until the early hours. At around 4am though, Mary was woken by a loud, rattling breathing; it was coming from her husband, and when she lifted the lamp to see if he was alright, his face was blackened with bruises. The next thing Rose MacCoag, apparently sleeping in an adjoining room, knew was that Mary had run to her crying "Rise, rise, for John's gone!". While Rose went to the other bedroom, Mary ran outside in her nightclothes, and straight to the next door cottage, where John's boss, Charlie MacMillan, lived. She came back with Mrs. MacMillan and their daughter, but by the time they returned, John certainly looked dead.

At some stage soon after this, Mary MacCoag had evidently tried to make John more comfortable, dead though he seemed to be. She tried to shift him around in the bed, and when her brother Donnie arrived at the cottage, he found her trying to drag John actually back into the bed. Mary told him that he'd half-fallen out, but as fast as she got one limb back in bed, another fell out. Clearly poor John MacCoag was unconscious by then, and couldn't have been trying to get out of the bed by himself, but pulling and manhandling him around as best she could at the time, if there had been any life left in him, did she inadvertently finish him off by breaking his neck or his back, when he was already so badly injured that all it took was a quick twist? It's not a nice thought and at the time, Donnie insisted that she send for the doctor. Someone however had sent for the schoolmaster, Mr. MacNeil, and when he arrived (John's face must have still been black with bruises) all he said was that MacCoag was just sleeping off the whisky he'd had earlier, and that he would be "quite well in the morning". He even took his pulse and declared it "regular" and firm. Sadly, in those days before the general public were aware of not feeling for someone else's pulse with their own thumb, the schoolmaster was probably feeling his own pulse coming from John McCoag's lifeless wrist!

With such advice to comfort her, Mary MacCoag went back to bed, although her brother was still unhappy. It was only later that same morning, when there was no change in John, that Donnie managed to persuade his sister to send for young Dr. Orr. John's boss agreed, and loaned a horse to Donnie and the young man set off at what could only have been a furious gallop for the village.

It took Dr. Orr half an hour to ride to Gartvain, probably as fast as he could, but by the time he arrived of course, his patient was certainly dead, and had been so for several hours it seemed. Dr. Orr spoke to the family extensively, to find out how it had all happened, and they related the tale of the shinty match, the fight, the walk home, and the events of the previous evening.

With nothing else to do that day, and presumably after the doctor had left, the family stripped John's body and prepared him as best they could, for what was to come. Whether Dr. Orr had mentioned that other events would be happening before John's funeral or not, is unknown, but that same afternoon, word had got round the parish sufficiently enough for several local worthies to gather at the minister's house to go and look at the body. Dr. Orr wasn't comfortable about being the only medic present and would have preferred another to witness any preliminary examination he made, but the other men wanted the doctor to get on with it. Perhaps the others wanted to be certain John was actually dead, so they could apply for the arrest warrants.[13]

Meanwhile, the two proponents of the attack on John MacCoag were still in the parish, and must have been getting anxious when they heard what had happened over at Gartvain. One of them, Duncan MacMillan, called at a friend's house and seemed remorseful, telling the other man how although he remembered hitting MacCoag, he was aware that he hadn't done so intending him to die. Duncan MacDougall however, the father of the illegitimate baby[14] and the main protagonist in the affray, was subsequently accosted by Mary MacCoag's brother. Of course in a place with such a close community spirit as Southend has, any differences between neighbours are more magnified than in urban areas, so it can't have come as a surprise to Duncan MacDougall to be castigated, yet again, by Mary's brother. By that time, MacMillan and MacDougall must have been fearing a visit from the sheriff's men up at Campbeltown, but for the moment, all that was happening in Southend was that a post mortem exam was performed on John MacCoag's body. He had indeed suffered a massive head injury as a result of the strike from Duncan MacDougall's shinty stick; there was a cut above his left ear, the skin on his head was swollen, there was extensive bruising throughout and his brain was suffused with blood. In sensitivity possibly to the family, Dr. Orr declared that there wasn't an excessive smell of alcohol about him, and none evident in his stomach.

In the coming weeks, the authorities started work at the prosecution and by early April, the messenger at arms had come to Southend to apprehend MacMillan and MacDougall at their respective farms. The messenger however was thwarted – neither man was to be found, and although the summons was left with their servants at the farmhouses, they were gone for good, to Ireland so the local rumour said.[15]

Nevertheless, a trial had to go ahead, and so it did on Friday the 22nd April at Inveraray, before the Circuit Court Advocate, Lord Murray (a born legal eagle with an estate on Loch Fyne, and renowned for his hospitality and support of the common man[16]) and the usual panoply of court officials, and a host of witnesses. With some 49 of these, all from Southend,[17] it must have been quite a sight for the Inveraray folk to see such quantities of strangers, with their Kintyre accents, if not Gaelic, turn up at Crown Point. They'd probably have only just fitted into the building, waiting for their turn in court to testify, but it must have been a reassurance to Mary MacCoag to see so many people turn up to support her.

With no-one to put in the dock of course, all that could be done in court that day was listen to the lengthy witness statements, and declare the two Duncans outlaw. A notice was put on the market cross at Campbeltown and the same messenger at arms who'd come looking for MacDougall and MacMillan earlier in the month, loudly announced their criminality one Sunday morning,[18] just at the time when the locals would be going to kirk; a surefire way of getting the message heard!

Mary McCoag meanwhile had had to go back to Gartvain without a bread winner, and possibly three children to be supported. Her future may therefore have been tenuous, but the community spirit at Southend clearly wasn't. The same family who'd supported her at the time of John's death would also have stood by her in the days afterwards, and the old records give testimony to that support from the community. So many times in such circumstances, widows disappear into the city, become homeless and have to go on the road, hawking, or in later decades go into a workhouse. For a formerly married woman, possibly with children, the future was bleak; not in Southend it wasn't. Just five years later, Mary MacCoag was gainfully employed in Campbeltown, living alongside her fellow Irish-borns and amongst people whose surnames were common in Southend.[19] By the time of the next census, fifteen years after her husband's death, she was back home in Southend, working as a children's nurse for a local farmer whose wife had died recently.[20] Both Mary and the farmer and children had disappeared from all the old records by the time of the next census, and with no headstone or death register for any of them (the farmer's wife has a headstone), they may have gone abroad or to Ireland or down south.

Despite the work done on Carskey beach in recent decades, Southend remains in many ways the same as it was on the day when John died. Although Gartvain is now no more than a single building down a farm track, many of the other farms are still there and still working; fences are mended, cattle are fed, fields are ploughed, and there remains still a community spirit in this place on the edge of the ocean.

The old shinty field still sits by the beach, the latter frequented by locals, although shinty is no longer played there. As a sport it has a doubtful future in Kintyre, although the womens' and junior teams are thankfully keeping the game alive in the area.[21] As vigorous a sport as shinty remains (and long may it remain), with modern safety precautions, hopefully no-one, in Kintyre or beyond, will again suffer as John MacCoag did.

FOOTNOTES

1. "Camanachd! The Story of Shinty" by Roger Hutchinson, published Birlinn Ltd, Edinburgh, 2004, pp. 6,8,9,11,12,14 etc.
2. JC26/1836/270; JC13/56, available in the National Records of Scotland historic search room, Edinburgh.
3. timeanddate.com; tides.willyweather.co.uk; the tide was coming in at the time, but would have only been half way.
4. JC26/1836/270; JC13/56, available in the National Records of Scotland historic search room, Edinburgh.
5. "Camanachd! The Story of Shinty" by Roger Hutchinson, published Birlinn Ltd, Edin 2004, p.32; JC26/1836/270; JC13/56, available in the National Records of Scotland historic search room, Edinburgh.
6. JC26/1836/270; JC13/56, available in the National Records of Scotland historic search room, Edinburgh.
7. "Camanachd! The Story of Shinty" by Roger Hutchinson, published Birlinn Ltd, Edinburgh 2004, p.32.
8. JC26/1836/270; JC13/56, available in the National Records of Scotland historic search room, Edinburgh.
9. Ibid.
10. Encyclopaedia Britannica, Macropaedia, published Encyclopaedia Britannica 1975, USA, volume 12, pp.1054-56.
11. JC26/1836/270; JC13/56, available in the National Records of Scotland historic search room, Edinburgh.
12. Ibid.
13. Ibid. It's also worth mentioning that in the trial notes, there's an account written by Dr. Orr describing how he attended Gartvain on what appears to be the 17th January and found MacCoag alive, but very ill. This can only be a mix up, perhaps with McIlvery's sickness after being hit during the fight, or even a mix up with the dates, as John McCoag was well dead and had been autopsied

by Dr. Orr himself on the 17th.

14. Baptisms, Southend parish, Old Parish Registers, August 1832, Barbara, illegitimate daughter to Jean O'May and Duncan MacDougall, available on scotlandspeople.com

15. JC26/1836/270; JC13/56, available in the National Records of Scotland historic search room. Edinburgh.

16. en.wikipedia.org; www.nationalgalleries.org

17. JC26/1836/270; JC13/56, available in the National Records of Scotland historic search room, Edinburgh.

18. time &date.com; JC26/1836/270, available in the National Records of Scotland historic search room, Edinburgh.

19. Census Return 1841, Lorn street Campbeltown, available on scotlandspeople.com There is another Mary McCoag of a similar age to John's wife, at Bailevianan in 1841. Living with her is an 8 year old John MacCoag, the name and approximate age of one of John and Mary's children, but that Mary isn't specified as being a widow, and she's of "Independent" means. Was she perhaps another sister or cousin of John's, raising young John to allow his mum to go to work in the town?

20. Census Return, 1851, parish of Southend, available on scotlandspeople.com

21. en.wikipedia.org/wiki/Kintyre_Camanachd

SIX

The first quarter of the 19th century, with its repeated social unrest (including the Radical Rebellion which had so unnerved the authorities at the time of the Kilchrenan whisky riot) was a disturbing time for the powers-that-be all over the country. There was a lack of conformity in security services, a lack of adequate laws to back up what little conformity there was, and the hands of various committees were tied when they tried to prevent such social and civic problems as the Radical Rebellion. There'd been moves fairly early on to try to redress these difficulties, and Glasgow and Edinburgh had of course long had their own efficient police forces. The rest of the country however also badly needed something which would make it easy for every burgh and every county to set up their own police force without having to fight their way through parliament. There was one law passed which made it easier for certain districts to do this, but it wasn't until the Rogue Money Act of 1839 that the rest of the Scotland was able to follow suit.[1]

In Argyll the reaction to the new Parliamentary Act, was for 16 local lairds, gentry and notables to meet one April day in 1840 to discuss the prospect of starting a constabulary for the county. Their first task was to appoint a superintendent and adverts went into a couple of national newspapers, drawing an apparently suitable man from Berwickshire who started work the following July, hitting the ground running by appointing and meeting constables and all sorts of other officials. Efforts were made to contact neighbouring police forces to establish boundaries, details of the constables' duties were drawn up, their wages decided on, and the rather idealised principle of a "chain of command stretching from one end of the county to the other" posited. The ten original constables were stationed everywhere from Campbeltown to Dunoon, Oban, Taynuilt and several places in between, with some sent to Islay and Mull. The new Superintendent had presumably, on the Board's advice, done a tour of the county to see what he was up against, but none of the men could imagine what was ahead of them.[2]

The new Argyll 'police constables' of 1840 were issued with uniforms (a black swallow-tailed coat, trousers and a tall, reinforced hat [3]) and paid the wages applicable to an artisan of 14 shillings a week, being expected however at first to serve pretty much 24 hours a day, 7 days a week.[4] With precious little respect for the former parish constables however, the new police constables had little chance of getting any respect at all. As hard as most of them probably worked, they hadn't been employed for their skill in accounting and clerical matters, so their lateness in sending in reports and receipts for their wages soon started to cause havoc with the Committee. As the months went on, all sorts of other problems began slowing up the day to day work of the Board, while any system of hierarchy was almost non-existent. The PCs, out on a limb as they were, were getting told what to do by anyone who thought they were in charge – and the PC got the blame for it! Left largely to their own devices, without even batons or handcuffs at first, and certainly no office or other premises, it's natural the men took matters into their own hands. Also naturally, some were fond of strong drink, some invented their own working hours and techniques, and equally naturally, there was all hell to pay when the 'Super' came a-calling! Some men were dismissed after a few months, some reprimanded, some replaced by ones from elsewhere in the county, and it's no surprise that, like other areas of the UK, the first efforts at this new Police Force weren't met with very positive opinions from the populace.[5]

By the end of 1843, the Committee seemed to be meeting in Lochgilphead, where there was a constable, Hugh Livingstone, in January the following year.[6] At the time, Lochgilphead had risen from the one-street village of the turn of the 18th and 19th centuries, into a small but thriving town, bolstered by the popularity of the Crinan Canal. It had risen further even than it had done by the time the lady coin-smashers were peddling their fake shillings around the shops in 1829, and there was a "mischievously great" number of inns and alehouses, some banks, cattle fairs, a clothing society, imports and exports via Ardrishaig, a kirk and meeting house, and a vigorous fishing trade with more than one slipway and boats repainted a different colour every year. There were also of course a few private schools, although no Kirk school at that time, the private ones being overseen by the laird at Achandarroch, who also insisted on having a hand in any new building propositions going up around the village. The main street was then, as now, Argyll street, running north to south with crossing roads at top and bottom and a few side roads leading out towards Kilmory. There was extensive farming and market garden and plant nursery land around, especially behind the west side of Argyll street, where stood the Stag Inn, opposed on the other side of the road, further down at the corner by the Argyll Inn. [7]

Quite where in this thriving little town on the edge of the Crinan Canal PC Hugh Livingstone was stationed isn't possible to tell, but it may have been not too far from the site of the current police station, which was at least a "gaol" three years later[8], and soon after the initial Police Board meeting, hosted future meetings of the committee.[9] Wherever Hughie's house was, it was there, early one January morning in 1844, that someone must have come with an urgent message; PC Livingstone's professional presence was required urgently at a small apartment in Argyll street, near to the Stag Hotel.[10]

Dugie MacMillan the proprietor there had been about his business that morning when he heard screaming from the accommodation, possibly above Bobby Martin's shop.[11] Dugie must have known that a local school teacher, Peter Campbell and his mother and maternal aunt lived there,[12] all Craignish people, and the teacher well respected in his home parish. The noises from Peter Campbell's flat however were desperate enough to make Dugie rush upstairs and start breaking the door down. Before he'd finished, there were other men there helping and the sight which greeted them inside would have been terrible to behold.

In the little flat, Peter Campbell was standing in his day clothes with an open razor in his hand and blood spattered over his trousers and socks. Unbeknown to the men at the door, the body of a woman was lying, probably in a bed in an adjoining room, while Peter's mother must have been in the vicinity, terribly injured, and perhaps collapsed on the floor near Peter, who was acting strangely, ranting and raving about witches and voices in his head telling him that he had to kill them. He was fighting the men at the door to get at the witches, but Dugie and the others managed to knock the razor out of his hand with a candlestick. Once this was done, they got hold of the teacher and made him secure, by which time, PC Livingstone may have arrived on the scene, and took matters in hand.[13]

With Peter thus apprehended, and away from the scene, one of the first things anyone did, was to send for a doctor to see if the lives of either victim could be saved. The women were sisters, Margaret and Mary MacDougall and in their sixties[14], the latter Peter's mother, and clearly happy, like in days of old, to use her maiden name as much as her married name. Her husband, Peter's father, had killed himself some time ago, back in Craignish, and the women had been living with the school-teacher for a few years by then, apparently contentedly enough.[15]

The doctor who'd been called to attend the sisters was John (or James) Hunter, the one who'd acted as JP when Peter MacDonald apprehended the women coin-smashers around the town in 1829. The report which Dr. Hunter later wrote (in his classic doctor's handwriting!) about what he found when he attended that little flat above Argyll street tells a tale of bloody tragedy. Margaret MacDougall, Peter's now-dead aunt, had a deep wound on the back of her neck, from ear to ear, almost cutting through her spinal cord. In addition to the severe neck wound, Margaret had others on the side of her neck, her left shoulder and the top of her head. As for Peter's mother, Mary Campbell, she was very badly wounded, so badly Dr. Hunter doubted if she would survive.[16] She had wounds on her neck, jaw, wrist, elbow, and brow, all inflicted by the razor. There isn't any way of telling whether she did survive, but it seems unlikely. What does appear likely is that Peter attacked his aunt from behind, but instead of reaching round and cutting her throat at the front, he tried to cut her head off from the back and bungled it. It's common apparently, for people who try to kill or dismember to make their first efforts at removing the head from behind, in actual fact the most difficult way.[17] Mary MacDougall's wounds may have come about when she tried to intervene with the attack on her sister and the wounds on her elbow and wrist clearly indicate that she'd fought for her life against her own son, managing to prevent him slitting her throat, again perhaps from behind, as it seems she was fully awake at the time because of her screams.

In custody at Hugh Livingstone's house, and eventually somewhat calmed, Peter Campbell couldn't believe what had happened. He was convinced he'd been attacking some witches, induced to do so by the voices in his head, and that the men who came to the door were preventing him from doing so, and he'd had to fight them to gain access to the evil women; he wanted to speak to his dear lady relatives, since he didn't believe what he'd been told.[18] It's to be hoped that Hughie Livingstone didn't have children of his own living in the house at the time, as one can only imagine the state of his prisoner that day, and the story Hughie had to tell his wife when they arrived on the doorstep.

The curiosity of Peter thinking his mother and aunt were witches, at this late date isn't quite so unusual when one considers the local situation. Over on the edge of the Canal, probably in North Knapdale parish, one oldie (known locally as "Sarah of the Bog") was often consulted by the locals and appeased by gifts of whisky. Sarah lived alone in a wee cottage and was generally acknowledged to be a witch, although one suspects she was more of a 'wise woman' and it may have been the very children whom Peter taught who gossiped about her. She was later found dead, partly in her own fireplace, and the issue of witches in the 19th century wasn't so unusual.[19]

From custody in Lochgilphead, under the hands of Hugh Livingstone, Peter Campbell was transferred to Inveraray the following day, probably by Hughie himself, perhaps on a boat hired for the purpose; the Campbeltown PC for example had to take arrested criminals to Inveraray himself, and one would imagine it would have been quicker by boat.[20]

Incarcerated in the prison on Crown Point at Inveraray, Peter Campbell still couldn't understand what had happened. Someone else must have done this terrible thing, he thought, if indeed it was all true. He actually requested paper, pen, and ink to write a letter, in his neat but heavy handwriting, to a friend, a merchant, in Lochgilphead, and actually one of the ones who'd intervened during the incident, begging the man to bail him out of jail without delay, so he could find whoever had accused him of this awful act. His signature was somewhat shaky.[21]

The letter Peter wrote still exists, but it was never delivered; there was no chance of anyone bailing him out, and clearly the authorities had read and confiscated it before it reached the postie. He still believed that it had been witches whom he'd attacked, not his dear lady relatives, and so he still believed in jail. Another of his alter egos was clearly to the fore now.[22]

By the time Peter was imprisoned at Inveraray, the fine court house and debtors' prison opened in 1820, had seen more than enough activity. The old cells below the court room had been abandoned for the male prisoners, and they were now accommodated on the lower floor of the separate prison block with the women above them on the top floor. Across at the other side of the prison grounds, a fine new cell block, complete with service rooms, sanitary provision and chimnies, was being built, destined to house the male prisoners, while the debtors would eventually be housed on the very top storey of the court house.[23] There were very few other prisoners in the jail when Peter first came and within ten days of his committal, one violent criminal left.[24] In future months and years, prisoners convicted of other violent assaults, house breaking, theft and (in a couple of tragic cases) women accused of killing their newborn babies all spent a few months or just over a year behind the Inveraray bars, with one man sent to transportation.[25] Peter was clearly imprisoned in a cell by himself; no prison authority would want to house another criminal in the same cell as a murderer with such an unhinged mind, and it's not known if he was ever transferred to the new prison block.[26]

For the time being however, Peter Campbell faced his trial in the fine semi-circular courthouse on Crown Point one April day in 1844. One could imagine the little court house was full that day, and the stress and the change in surroundings which presented themselves to Peter must have had an effect on his mental state.

Despite the lack of extant witness statements from the trial, the long list of witnesses tells its own story. Aside from the usual officials, giving evidence as per normal practise (the Fiscal, the Sheriff Substitute, the clerk and an apprentice), the men who'd broken down Peter's door also stood in court and told the story about what had happened. Crucially, Peter's badly injured mother was also included on the list, although whether she lived to stand in court, let alone whether she was allowed to testify against her son, is debateable. There were several doctors and surgeons on the list, including one from Craignish, and another Craignish man who may have been a relative, and a few more townsmen. Despite the lack of witness statements available to historians, the testimonies of the various doctors who examined Peter in jail do exist.

One of these was the prison doctor, Mr. King, and he was of the opinion that Peter had a "strong hereditary disposition to insanity". Peter's father's suicide out at Craignish is mentioned, and both his mother and aunt displayed symptoms of a "weak mind". This same doctor saw Peter repeatedly over the coming months and years and although Dr. King's patient appears to have improved in time, there was still some doubt about Peter's suitability for release. The school-teacher had an "exceedingly excitable temperament", suffered from delusions, and had episodes of insanity lasting two or three days, inspired by strong drink, opposition to his wishes or some other "exciting" cause. He advised that Peter be kept under "proper restraint", or else he'd be dangerous to society. Other medics later also testified to Peter's unstable state of mind, and all these symptoms do make one wonder if he suffered from some sort of schizophrenia or disassociative identity disorder, difficult even in modern times to diagnose correctly. Whatever he had, he clearly needed something more than a jail cell. Unfortunately, for the time being, a jail cell at Inveraray was all he was likely to get, and clearly the verdict in court that April day at Inveraray couldn't be anything other than criminally insane.[27]

Back in the Campbells' home parish of Craignish, people who knew the family, especially Peter, soon found out about the tragedy. All they knew of their friend was that he was a skilled, well-thought of, teacher, and some 117 residents and elders got together a petition, appealing for something to be done to relieve his distress. Could he be released from jail, they asked, or if not, could he be put into an asylum such as Perth prison, where he could teach the prisoners. Or perhaps he could at least not be kept in solitary confinement. This appeal, well-intentioned but misguided, sparked off another wave of investigations into Peter's case. The prison board at Inveraray were certainly unable to authorise his release or transferral, and they replied that Peter's case would have to be transferred to Edinburgh. As a result of this, more doctors' reports were called up, with more doctors visiting him in his cell. Two of these, including a man who'd known him for 20 years already, described how his mental condition varied over the days, and he sometimes did indeed appear sane, but would easily slip into what we might call a paranoid and violent state of mind, by some sudden turn of events. The jailor at Inveraray was also asked to make a statement and all the paperwork was sent to Edinburgh to be considered by the Court of Justiciary. The answer which came back must have been the expected one – Peter's release or transferral was refused.

With the decision by higher authorities barring Peter from being relieved of his distress, one might have assumed his case had the proverbial red line drawn beneath it. However two years after being taken to Inveraray, Peter left the town, (not under his own steam of course), to another prison 80 miles away.[28]

Back in 1844, when the people of Craignish had appealed for Peter's transferral, they'd mentioned Perth prison. This place in the middle of the town still stands and is still used as a penal institution. It had first been built in 1810-12 to hold French prisoners of war, although by Peter's time, with various changes of governor and structural alterations, it was holding civilian prisoners. In 1843 it was said to occupy a "fine situation", with "magnificent" architecture and several auxiliary buildings, "forming altogether a considerable village", with the prisoners occupying high arched, relatively spacious cells.[29] For the ordinary inmates at Perth however, their time was governed by a combination of the 'Separate' and 'Silent' systems, whereby the prisoners were barred from being able to communicate with, hear or view each other, even while at Sunday services in the chapel. The theory was that, left to an effective solitary confinement, they would ponder the cause of their incarceration and come to be responsible, remorseful citizens, not erring again. To this end, there were only small airing yards in the prison and the inmates occupied their time with the traditional manual labour, picking oakum or doing pointless exercises, which however left them exhausted at the end of the day, probably unable to protest much against the warders, who were nevertheless encouraged to be more than the cold, unforgiving brutes of former centuries.[30] As for the prisoners judged criminally insane, Perth was acknowledged at the time as amongst the very best in Scotland for housing such people and one hopes that they were treated rather more compassionately than those not judged mentally ill.

Peter Campbell, as one of these criminally insane, was admitted to the wards at Perth prison in July 1846. He was recorded whilst at Inveraray as being of "superior education" and earning the prison a profit of 6d a week from his fishing net-making skills,[31] so he presumably found similar employment at Perth. He was still there at the time of the 1851 census, but one morning in May, six years later, with his "constitution broken down from the effect of insanity for some years", and still classed as a "lunatic prisoner", he died.[32] The prison doctor had seen him the day before, and the phrase "broken down from the effect of insanity" isn't very specific; did Peter just give up on life, or was it a euphemism for suicide, such synonyms occasionally being used for describing suicide on a death certificate, in this instance one hopes out of respect for the person's memory rather than fear of the prison authorities investigating an inmate gaining access to, perhaps, a rope. Whatever the truth of the matter, Peter Campbell, the former schoolmaster from the Argyll coast, was buried within the prison grounds, his grave undoubtedly undisturbed still among the rebuilt and built over sections of the prison precincts.[33] Back home in Argyll, his mother and aunt were probably buried in the old cemetery out at Kilmory, or perhaps back home in Craignish, or at Kilmichael Glassary, neither of their graves now identifiable, and clearly therefore without any family left to commemorate them.

By that time in Argyll, the criminal face of the whole county had changed drastically from what it was at the beginning of the century. There was a new Duke in Inveraray, a new Superintendent for the police, offices and officers distributed all over the county, in uniform and with regulation issue truncheons and handcuffs. There were new judges in the court, the chaplain now held services in the prison corridors, rather than walk the miserable inmates up Main street to the kirks and even the debtors were settled into their new accommodation on the top floor of the court house.[34] With all these improvements in the face of justice and tackling criminality in the county, and despite the rumblings of Rebellion in earlier decades, criminality appears to have changed aswell. Although murders still occasionally happened, and the population had risen, there remained only a mere fraction of that population convicted or accused of murder, at least in Argyll. Thefts, poachings, breaches of the peace, arsons and assaults still continued as rife as before, but something was clearly having an influence on the worst criminals of Argyll.[35]

In Glasgow in the same era, there was a similarly tiny fraction of the population convicted of such serious crimes, but crucially that figure appears to have been twice the level of Argyll's figure.[36] Could it have been the greater powers of the police in Glasgow, among city streets, with easier access to criminals, which brought more murderers to book? Did the huge rural population in Argyll, and the vast areas that often a single officer had to cover mean that our serious criminals just got away with it? If that was the case, one would expect record of outlawry, and perhaps subsequent crimes to have arisen in the old court records; unless of course the criminals exported themselves to Glasgow and changed their name, hence the higher crime rate there! Alternatively, with the difficulty of housing convicted murderers until at least the new prison block was built, did the Inveraray courts simply prefer to write off such cases as culpable homicide? Like with the MacPhail brothers back in 1831, we'll probably never know the true reason for the low level of recorded serious crime in Argyll in the middle of the 19th century.

Whatever the reason behind this curiously low murder rate, like at the turn of the previous century, the attitude to crime from society was changing. The Victorians had a thirst for spilt blood and news about serious crime, and when hangings did occur in towns other than Inveraray, until such occasions were banned from being public gatherings, vast crowds would still gather to witness the event. But laws were being brought in to ensure prison conditions were more just, and the ease of transport and communications surely made it easier for witnesses and victims to report crimes. The old days had passed, arguably in a way never experienced before, and with more changes to come in future decades (railways, telegraph, electricity, photography etc) the old ways had gone with them; if it meant only half the murders which Glasgow was experiencing, surely all to the good.

FOOTNOTES

1. www.inverness-courier.co.uk; british-police-history.uk
2. CA/1/8, Minute Book 1, available in Argyll & Bute County archives ("Live Argyll"), Manse Brae, Lochgilphead.
3. Ibid., pp.17-18,31,39, 52,101, 127 etc; testimony of Liam Bowler, Metropolitan Police Heritage Service to who the author is indebted.
4. CA/1/8, Minute Book 1, available in Argyll & Bute County archives ("Live Argyll"), Manse Brae, Lochgilphead.
5. Ibid., pp. 118,129; Minute book 2: pp.16, 18, 28, 34-35,39, 40 (and

other references), 113 etc.

6. Ibid, Minute Book 2, end of 1843.

7. "The Second Statistical Account", vol.7, Renfrew-Argyll, published Blackwood & Sons, Edinburgh 1845, pp.691-699; early OS map, available on maps.nls.uk

8. Admiralty map of 1847, available on maps.nls.uk

9. CA/1/8, Minute Book 2, available in Argyll & Bute County archives ("Live Argyll"), Manse Brae, Lochgilphead.

10. JC26/1844/242 available in the National Records of Scotland historic search room, Edinburgh.

11. Census Return, 1841, Lochgilphead, Argyll street, available on scotlandspeople.com

12. Ibid.

13. JC26/1844/242 available in the National Records of Scotland historic search room, Edinburgh; Glasgow Herald newspaper, 15 January 1844, p.2, available in Special Collections, Mitchell Library, Glasgow.

14. Census Return, 1841, Lochgilphead, Argyll street, when each woman is stated to be in her 60s.

15. JC26/1844/242, available in the National Records of Scotland historic search room, Edinburgh.

16. Ibid.

17. "All that remains, a life in death" by Sue Black, published Penguin Random House, London 2019, p.202.

18. JC26/1844/242 available in the National Records of Scotland historic search room, Edinburgh.

19. "The Whisky Distilleries of the United Kingdom", by Alfred Barnard, published David and Charles Reprints, 1969, from original print of 1887, p.124.

20. CA/1/8, Minute Book 2, available in Argyll & Bute County archives ("Live Argyll"), Manse Brae, Lochgilphead.

21. JC26/1844/242, available in the National Records of Scotland historic search room, Edinburgh.

22. Ibid.

23. The Royal Commission on the Ancient and Historical Monuments of Scotland volume 7, Mid Argyll and Cowal, medieval and later monuments published 1992, pp.445-448.

24. Neil Smith, JC26/1843/275 & AD14/43/307, available in the National Records of Scotland historic search room in Edinburgh.

25. The several sources and documents include JC26/1844/235, JC26/1844/237, JC26/1845/235, JC26/1845/317, JC26/1846/201 and others, available in the National Records of Scotland historic search room in Edinburgh.

26. JC26/1844/242 available in the National Records of Scotland historic search room, Edinburgh.

27. rethink.org/advice-and-information and https//psychcentral. com; JC26/1844/242, available in the National Records of Scotland historic search room, Edinburgh.

28. JC26/1844/242 available in the National Records of Scotland historic search room, Edinburgh.

29. institutionalhistory.com; testimony of Grace Woolmer, Perth and Kinross Heritage Trust, to whom the author is indebted.

30. "Shades of the prison house" by Harry Potter, published The Boydell Press, Woodbridge, 2019, pp.204-211.

31. JC26/1844/242 available in the National Records of Scotland historic search room, Edinburgh.

32. Peter's death certificate, 1857, available on scotlandspeople.com

33. Testimony of Grace Woolmer, Perth and Kinross Heritage Trust, to whom the author is indebted; the early OS maps available on maps.nls.uk.

34. "A History of Clan Campbell", volume 3, by Alastair Campbell of Airds, published Edinburgh University Press, 2004, pp.294-298; "Inveraray Jail, County Prison of Argyll, 1820-1889" (guide book of Inveraray Jail Museum), published Landmark Press, p.31; CA/1/8, Minute books 1 and 2, available in Argyll & Bute County archives ("Live Argyll"), Manse Brae, Lochgilphead; The Royal Commission on the Ancient and Historical Monuments of Scotland volume 7, Mid Argyll and Cowal, medieval and later monuments published 1992, pp.445-448.

35. CA/1/8, Minute Book 1, p.87, available in Argyll & Bute County archives ("Live Argyll"), Manse Brae, Lochgilphead; the online catalogue of the National Records of Scotland historic search room, where detail can be had of various such crimes in Argyll around this era.

36. The author's calculations based on population figures for Argyll and Glasgow (dittobooks.co.uk/extras/census-population-1801-1851 and jstor.org/stable/pdf/2337739.pdf) compared with numbers of murders in Glasgow in 1841 and 1851 (available on the NRS online catalogue). The murder rate for Argyll on these two dates however is nil, so the author has used an average of 0.9 for each of these respective years, since there were nine murders between 1840 and 1850 in Argyll. Such calculations work out as approximately 0.0025% of the Glasgow population convicted of murder in 1851 and 0.0011% of the same for Argyll in the same year.